HOW TO SURVIVE
THE TERRIBLE TWOS

HOW TO SURVIVE
THE TERRIBLE TWOS

Diary of a mother under siege

 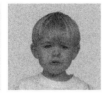

CAROLINE DUNFORD

Editors Richard Craze, Roni Jay

new tricks for old dogs

Published by White Ladder Press Ltd
Great Ambrook, Near Ipplepen, Devon TQ12 5UL
01803 813343
www.whiteladderpress.com

First published in Great Britain in 2005

10 9 8 7 6 5 4 3 2

ISBN 0 9548219 3 9

British Library Cataloguing in Publication Data
A CIP record for this book can be obtained from the British Library.

Designed and typeset by Julie Martin Ltd
Cover design by Julie Martin Ltd
Cover photographs by Jonathon Bosley
Printed and bound by TJ International Ltd, Padstow, Cornwall

White Ladder Press
Great Ambrook, Near Ipplepen, Devon TQ12 5UL
01803 813343
www.whiteladderpress.com

DEDICATION

There are lot of people I want to mention here: the Emperor's friends and family for being there and loving him; my own parents whose jobs as parents I am only now beginning to appreciate; the friends who stick by me even in the most tantrum filled and dark days (you know who you are – the puddings, the emails and the hugs); the Emperor's devoted godfather; Rachel Weinstein, MD (board certified pediatrician) for answering endless questions with patience, humour and the utmost professionalism; Carolyn Westwood, health visitor, for adding her invaluable tips and advice; the mothers who shared their stories; Roni and Rich for editing and publishing this, but most of all I need to thank the Emperor's father for travelling this road with me, always being there, always being supportive and always loving us (even when we're both being very difficult); and also our incredible son, who I adore and who remains my greatest challenge and my greatest inspiration.

DISCLAIMER

This is a book written for parents by a parent. While every effort has been made to check all facts, it is not a book by an expert, but by a mother under siege and offers only the advice one parent might give to another.

INFORMATION PANELS

INTRODUCTION

This book is a diary of my experiences of living and learning with my son as he progressed from two years old to three years old or, as this is better known, through the Terrible Twos.

I hope all parents will identify with the journal entries and find these not only entertaining but also reassuring, support-ive and funny. The journal is interspersed with information panels, which are fully indexed at the back of the book. So in cases of dire need you can go straight to the topics that are currently besetting you; be that toilet training, fussy eating, tantrums or sleeping problems.

When you do come to the information panels you will see they are not academic words of wisdom delivered by a professional sitting behind a desk. They are very much the knowledge gained as a mother under siege. They contain all the things I wish I had known earlier.

But first I should introduce us.

MEET THE EMPEROR AND ME

In my twenties I wrote for newspapers, worked in some terri-ble offices, cajoled people into publishing my fiction, and almost as an afterthought trained as a psychotherapist and counsellor. Then, when I'm well into enjoying the playground of my thirties, my son arrives. At this point, I'm under the delusion that I'm a fairly clued up individual, who has worked with people going through some of the worst crises of their lives, and nothing much can faze me.

Excuse me, while I roll around on the floor in hysterical laughter at my hideous naivety.

My world is not upside down. It has entered a series of entirely new dimensions.

I wouldn't have missed these first two years for anything, but they have been (how can I put this delicately?) challenging. I adore him. I would do anything to protect him. But sometimes it's all I can do not to shred the furniture when he refuses (yet again) to eat the carefully prepared banquet of a thousand and one flavours, preferring instead to wear it in his newly washed hair.

According to the Great Emperor, who is my son:

- He is the centre of the universe.
- Everyone loves him.
- His Imperial Seneschal, Stinky Bear, never needs to be washed.
- He has a fascination for blondes (grown-up variety) and lady-babies.
- Imperative to his happiness are his own mobile phone, an endless supply of pudding and never knowingly to eat a vegetable.
- I am the best mother in the world and the worst (especially the worst when I won't give him whatever dangerous thing he is currently lusting after).

According to his mother, the Great Emperor:

- Is the most wonderful baby in the world, and everyone

should love him. (From the moment the hospital photographer squeaked in delight at the James Bond position he adopted for his first ever photo, I've known he was not only an unusually photogenic baby, but loves playing to an audience.)

- Despite his angelic looks, is as scheming and manipulative as a master politician.
- May not have spoken language, but he understands a great deal and has a will of iron.
- Cannot survive on an endless diet of puddings. He needs to eat vegetables, and he can't have a functional mobile phone to irradiate himself with.

and

- I am the best mother I can be.

Somehow over the next year, I must scale the mountain of excellent child rearing, while retaining some existence in my own right.

MY GOALS

1 By the time he is three the Emperor will be eating a healthy mixed diet without complaint, and pudding bribes will be a thing of the past.

2 Nappies will be a dim memory, with all bodily waste products going in the loo, without having to go through the hell of pottydom.

3 Every night the Emperor will go down for at least 10 hours of undisturbed rest.

4 As mother I will continually strive to provide entertainment and activities suitable for the Emperor's developing mind

and body (which includes an ethically correct selection of toys and television programs).

5   I will begin the socialisation process of the Emperor by finding him other children to play with, and cease surrounding him totally with servile adults.

6   At the end of the year, the Emperor will be able to give his real name and address when asked, and will be fluent in conversational adult-speak.

7   I will ensure that the Emperor's surroundings are safe, and that we never have another occurrence of the collapsed babygate and the stairs.

8   I will undertake to school the Emperor in the ways of acceptable behaviour without resorting to corporal punishment, or anything that may entail long term therapy (for either of us) at a later date.

9   I will not work full time. I will devote huge amounts of each day to the caring of the Emperor and his environs, but I will also write, study and achieve a minimal level of social life.

10 I will not be a sucker for the Emperor's huge blue topaz eyes or other formidable weapons in his armoury of manipulation and cajolement.

THE EMPEROR'S GOAL

1   To bend the known universe to his will.

THE DIARY OF A
MOTHER UNDER SIEGE

10TH NOVEMBER (eve)

The Emperor's Birthday

Exhausted. Lying in a darkened room. Round and round in my head echoes the thought, how will I cope this year? It's only going to get worse.

11TH NOVEMBER

This morning things don't seem so bad. I've actually had some time to think as my little boy plays happily with his new train set. The big set has been put away for later; a huge, electrically propelled ride-on train with its own circular track. He was so excited yesterday by this final big present that he waved and yelled "bye-bye!" as he whizzed round and round, increasingly confused by the never changing scenery.

By the evening the jolly Emperor had metamorphosed into a squalling creature from the abyss – too much fun and ice cream cake. Today, either indigestion or overexertion has turned him into a placid, amiable toddler. I'm enjoying this while it lasts.

BIRTHDAY PARTIES

Although they can enjoy the day tremendously few two year olds have any idea of what a birthday is. This is a day for grandparents, aunts and uncles (official and unofficial) to dote, and for parents to feel proud. Realistically, the chances of your child remembering this birthday when they are much older is slight. Therefore do not let yourself be drawn into a keeping up with what the other mothers/fathers at the local playgroup/ nursery/neighbourhood do. It's a day for celebration: do not make it unnecessarily painful.

Cameras

Using a camcorder or camera to record the day is a lovely idea, but ask someone else to use it for you. Being stuck behind either apparatus separates you from the action, and more importantly when your child looks back at this day one of the people they will really want to see is you.

12ᵀᴴ NOVEMBER

I'm fairly certain it is not a good idea to allow a toddler to consume his body weight in birthday chocolate. I'm consoling myself with the thought that at least it is good quality chocolate, full of milk, free from preservatives, but there's no getting away from the sugar content. The Emperor and I are struggling with food. He'll only use a spoon for pudding, otherwise it's finger food, and he'd rather eat the contents of the cat's litter tray than touch a vegetable. Which leaves me with Yorkshire puddings, toasties (that he picks bits out of), cheese (melted, toasted or dipping) and bread.

I don't need to ask my health visitor to know this is not a good thing. This is what I wrote about my latest experience, the

Emperor's 23 month check up. It sums up my relationship with mine.

Firstly, she shows concern that he isn't yet voicing his needs, and talks to me about how important it will be for him to see a speech therapist, if he doesn't improve by nursery time (at three). At this point I interrupt, picking up her briefly mentioned point that it's early days, and suggest that he isn't speaking often with me, because he doesn't need to. I explain I am doing my best not to anticipate his needs, but I've definitely allowed too much pointing and too much telepathy. I say I do understand where this is coming from. I get my first frosty smile. I'm one of those mothers who answers back.

I pass all the 'do I know how to take care of my child?' questions (safety, food, tantrums etc). Of course I know the theory. I know what I'm meant to do.

The Emperor is also unimpressed by the interview. He refuses to do any of his tests until offered a crayon, whereupon he tries to crayon everything in sight. I explain he doesn't like being tested. Just as she is finally about to mark down that he can't build bricks, the Emperor gives her a filthy look and quickly stacks all six bricks on top of each other.

The ace of shocks is handed to me when I leave. A leaflet explaining preschoolers should be given attention at least every 30 minutes, preferably every 10.

I reread the article several times to make sure I understand what is being suggested. This method of parenting would allow me to get to the bathroom occasionally, but forget the minimal level of housework I do, my writing and ever having a bath again. And then it strikes me; I'm obviously meant to work through the night.

My mother consolingly reads the Dr Spock she used for me down the phone. Written in the fifties a fair amount holds true and an equal amount would be discounted today.

I calm down. I check. The Emperor is healthy and usually very happy. He's beginning to speak. I know my health visitor was trying to do her best. I consider sending her a note explaining why her demands are unreasonable.

Here endeth the lesson on **everyone will tell you what to do**.

EVERYONE WILL TELL YOU WHAT TO DO

It is important to respect the advice of health professionals and child specialists, but all children are different. They progress at different rates. All parents are different too, and will be able to offer their children different things. If your child is safe, healthy, happy and thriving, you're doing OK. There is no manual for raising a child. And frankly looking after a toddler is hard enough without trying to please everyone else.

However, none of this changes my problems with the Emperor's eating habits. I feel very stuck with this. I continually offer him various foods, but he refuses. He doesn't want to try what's on my plate and I know any attempt to force him to eat things he doesn't feel ready to try or has decided he doesn't like will, in the long run, only make the battle harder. **In this (as in many areas of toddler raising) patience is your only weapon.**

A TODDLER'S DIETARY REQUIREMENTS

A couple of things to bear in mind

Young children need more fat than their adult counterparts; this provides energy in a more concentrated form than carbohydrates. So your toddler is encouraged to have full fat milk, ice

---

creams, and all those dairy things we love as adults and deny ourselves for health reasons.

Like us, children need starchy foods, fruit and vegetables and dairy/protein foods daily. As children grow they get more and more energy from starchy/carbohydrate intake, but all three areas are vital for healthy development. The key to ensuring this mix is flexibility. My son is currently vegetarian (with his GP's approval), and despite his picky ways gets what he needs from rusks (high in vitamins), full fat milk, cheese, real fruit juice (more vitamins) and other carbohydrates like bread. I'd love him to eat broccoli or Brussels sprouts, but he is healthy.

Forcing a child to eat something will only ever make them more finicky in their food habits.

- Toddlers need a number of small meals during the day. As well as breakfast, lunch and tea, mid-morning and mid-afternoon snacks of milk or juice and finger food like carrot sticks, grapes, raisins or breadsticks help keep them happy and active.

- If you want to keep meals a whole family affair make requested snacks near to meal times smaller, and larger if the next meal is a couple of hours away. Aim to sit together as a family for as many meals as possible. Offer your child very small amounts of the same family food that everyone else is having.

- The best way to tell if a toddler is eating the right amount is if they are growing appropriately. Generally toddlers are very good at self-regulating intake, and will eat what they need. If they don't eat much at one meal, they will make it up at another or with a snack.

- Making your child eat when they are not hungry sets up bad habits for life.

- Don't become visibly upset or concerned over 'picky' eating. Continue offering a mixture of healthy snacks. The more fuss you make over what your child does and doesn't eat, the more they are rewarded with attention for that behaviour, and the more they will persist.

- Avoid refusing a child pudding if they don't finish a main course. This makes pudding a reward, rather than simply another foodstuff. If you have a very picky eater or suspect your child is refusing main courses to get to pudding, either do not warn the child there will be pudding at this meal, or separate pudding times from main meals. If you need a pudding after meals because of others' dietary requirements (or general family revolt) ensure the pudding is a healthy one, like stewed apple, rather than chocolate cake, so you're happy for your toddler to eat it instead of a main course.

- Be very positive and encouraging of anything they eat, and ignore what hasn't been touched.

- You can be fun and inventive about the way you present food to your child. One parent's two year old asked for 'foot' for breakfast. They cut foot shapes out of toast and served them with jam; their child ate them delightedly.

- If your child especially likes chocolate, offer chocolate raisins.

- You can disguise fresh fruit by blending it with milk into a smoothie.

- Forewarn about upcoming meals, and remove toys and TV (even if only for 10 minutes) to concentrating on eating.

- If you're worried about your child's eating habits, make a list over several days of what they do eat. It may be a more balanced diet than you think.

- If your child is a big drinker they may be getting a lot of what they need in this way so they actually need less food. A toddler needs only about a pint of milk every 24 hours – more than this will reduce their need for solid food. Fruit squash drinks can be high in calories and, while this isn't always a good thing, if you have a faddy eater it does mean they're probably getting all the calories they need if they drink a lot.

- Above all, don't panic. Virtually all picky eaters are actually getting most of the nutrients they need one way or another.

For more information on how to encourage your child to eat healthily, take a look at **The Art of Hiding Vegetables** *Sneaky ways to feed your children healthy food* by Karen Bali and Sally Child, also published by White Ladder Press, at £7.99.

13TH NOVEMBER

The cooker engineer informs me I should have been able to replace a seal myself and that my cooker would work better if it were clean. His comments are interspersed with little laughs, so I'm not provided with the opening I need to slap him or jump on his foot. I consider saying I work from home and I have a toddler. I don't because he's obviously not a stay at home parent (unless they live in his van) and because I feel guilty. I should be keeping the house cleaner for my son.

I'm forgetting again that my son is healthy, happy and never ill. I'm ignoring the unpalatable truth that working from home, on more than one project, means I'm trying to hold down several jobs, while still being a decent cleaner and outstanding super mum.

A good friend emails me to say she paid for a self-cleaning

oven and, while she's never actually seen it get the Jiff out, that's what she expects.

This afternoon, I have the choice between playing trains (again) and putting the Emperor in his room while I clean.

There is more than gas-burners to life.

Woohoo! Woohoo!

HANDLING THE DOMESTIC CHALLENGE (BETTER THAN ME)

The so-secret-it's-blindingly-obvious secret is to keep on top of the housework. The reality is this is not always possible. Hygiene and safety issues around the areas your child plays or where food is prepared are a must – the rest can be left. No one likes living in a muddle, but quality time with your child is more important than a domestic palace.

Use large toy storage containers
Bucket drawers and boxes become increasingly important. It's all very well to try and avoid toys with bits, but your child will be given them by well meaning friends and family, and you'll also give in when you see something you think will capture their imagination. Big, easy to use containers make it easy to scoop up toys at the end of the day, and they allow little, less co-ordinated hands to help put things away too.

16TH NOVEMBER

I intended to buy a juicer today at the local retail park, but unfortunately many of the Sunday papers opened their magazine columns with the line 'Only 38 days to Christmas'. I doubt anyone read the rest. Only glad I didn't try to take the Emperor with me into the scrum. Thank goodness for Internet shopping.

SHOPPING

Lots of parents take their toddlers shopping. This isn't obligatory. On some days it provides an interesting change of scenery for both parent and child, on others it is simply a nightmare. If you normally take your car to the shops, consider the cost of petrol, wear and tear etc, as well as your sanity, against paying the occasional fiver for a supermarket to deliver to you (ordering by phone or Internet). It isn't the extravagant expense it might first appear, and one little van doing the rounds as opposed to lots of people going back and forth must be better for the environment. You may fondly remember those lazy days of window shopping and leisurely browsing, but this isn't an acceptable way to shop with a toddler. This is what you do when you give your child to your partner at the weekend and go out for a recreational shop and coffee with old friends.

With a toddler in tow you do a comprehensive list before you go, and execute the acquiring of goods with the precision of a SWAT operation. Necessary equipment includes a comforter for the journey (bear or blanket), a drink in a container and a snack (such as small cubes of cheese, raisins or grapes); which are obviously not shoplifted from the particular supermarket you are visiting. Avoid taking toys that have multiple parts with you, unless you want to spend most of your shopping time inspecting the supermarket floor.

Unless you're a masochist, don't go shopping when your child is tired, hungry or due for a nap.

How do you get your child to stay in the trolley?

Always strap your toddler into the trolley. It's safer, and it has the added advantage that if it becomes the accepted norm they'll be less inclined to object on the days when they feel like clambering around and generally causing mayhem.

Once you're in the supermarket there are many ways to make the experience more interesting for the child: naming items that go into the trolley; and for the more advanced even working out how things can be combined ('What do we need to go with bread? With cereal?'). Ask your child to find something on the shelf even if you can see it: 'Where are the eggs? Can you find them for me?'

While you never leave a teddy bear behind if, when you've reached the car park, or even the checkout, you discover you've forgotten a key item – forget it. Do not return to the shop; it simply isn't worth the hassle. Make your escape. Accept you have so much on your mind that you will forget things. This isn't a sign you are losing your sanity, but simply that every day is offering different challenges and that sometimes you won't be able to keep up with everything because you are human. This is the time for friends and partners to come into their own and save the day. You can do without anything except nappies, milk and baby wipes for the few hours it takes your partner to come home from work or your friend to fill the void.

Always put nappies, milk and baby wipes at the top of your shopping list – and keep back-up packets at home.

18TH NOVEMBER

We had a tantrum today. The kind of full on experience that only a few short centuries ago would have had me on the vellum to arrange for an exorcism. The tantrum seemed to be the result of him not being able to create enough sound. He had the evil talking telephone (which rolls its eyes and chatters as it creeps across the floor), a xylophone he kept picking up and throwing to the ground, and countless other squeak/flash/bing things he had pulled out of the toy chest. (He's positively psychic when it comes to picking noisy toy sessions to coincide with Mama's premenstrual headaches.) Needless to say when some of his toys were removed, he was not a happy bunny and called on the full possession of 'brat spirit'. **I need to be far stricter, fairer and consistent about how many toys he is allowed out at once.**

19ᵀᴴ NOVEMBER

The Emperor is at the stage were he likes to repeat phrases. This morning I was greeted by, "Uh-hun, tank ooo wery much", which floored me until I remembered we'd been discussing Elvis last night. A few weeks ago, I was sure I heard the Emperor utter a particularly choice and juicy swear word. I decided, not very seriously, to give him his own innocuous swear word 'fong'. After one repetition he has taken to it greatly, swinging Stinky Bear above his head like a bola and crying "Fong! Fong!" I can imagine (all too easily) him launching into his battle cry as he scatters future nursery playmates before him. I have created Genghis toddler.

Toilet training. I've just read 'Most children are toilet trained between $1^1/2$ and 2' in one of those helpful supermarket magazines. Fong. Fong. Fong. There are times when the Emperor seems very aware of his bodily functions and times when he appears to have no clue. (How this can be with some of the brick loaded nappies he creates, I don't know.) I know there is no point trying to train a toddler who has no idea of what is going on, but I'm feeling very inadequate again.

24TH NOVEMBER

The Emperor has taken to sleeping late. It's hard not to take advantage. I know small children find routine comforting, but if he needs to sleep? I love him more than I love life, but at the moment it's such a relief when he's asleep. Every waking moment he knows by some uncanny Imperial instinct exactly what he is not allowed to do or touch – so of course this is exactly what he does. He has more toys than Hamleys. Toys he will scream blue murder about, if I try to put enough away to check if the floor really is still there, but which he will otherwise totally ignore. A highlight yesterday was his stealing a gold watch, which had foolishly been left within his reach and attempting to fling it through the fireguard into the roaring fire. Fortunately his pitching arm isn't that strong – yet.

26TH NOVEMBER

Last night I was too tired to realise a toddler should not be running around until 4am. In the cold, hard light of day, it is perfectly obvious. Yesterday, the Emperor played happily all afternoon with his megablocks and an attendant slave. He was so happy and excited (and he'd stolen/cajoled some tiny pieces of high sugar fudge) that he forgot to have an afternoon nap. So at 6.10pm, as I was preparing the Imperial repast, he literally fell over, asleep on his feet. Ah, poor tot, I thought, little suspecting he would refuse to wake until 10pm. What was then meant to be a quick, warm bath before bed turned into water Olympics, followed by a track triathlon. All right, I thought, a few minutes by the fire, while wearing his Christmas red pyjamas and looking remarkably cute, will do no harm. *It was so not the right thing to do.* At 3.30am he was finally prepared to stay in his bed, albeit singing quietly to himself (loudly through the baby monitor). Around 4am, as I blurrily estimate it, he fell asleep. 8.30am this morning, he was up as bright and breezy as a valetudinarian returning from a summer on the Riviera, while I found myself trying to spoon coffee into the toaster.

BEDTIME ROUTINE

Toddlers need a bedtime routine. Even if your child doesn't want to go to bed he will learn to recognise that being taken to clean his teeth signifies the end of the day. A bedtime story is a useful marker. Baby books are a new industry. There are plenty of good, brightly coloured books for babies, and even some that deal with bedtime routines. Entering the terrible twos children become more aware of themselves as individuals. Life will be a whole lot easier if you establish boundaries early on. I have begun to indoctrinate the Emperor that when he hears me start *How Do Dinosaurs Say Good Night?* (by Jane Yolen and Mark Teague), he knows this is the last story of the evening and he needs to settle down. And it is always the last story no matter how much he pleads for more.

- Keep to a regular bedtime.

- Don't fall into the bad habit of allowing just a little more time.

- Do the getting ready for bed things in the same order each night.

- Allow enough time to say goodnight properly and read a story.

- Be consistent when you leave the room. Tuck your child in, cuddle them and leave. If they follow you put them back to bed again...and again...and again. Stay calm; if you get upset or angry this will reinforce your toddler's behaviour.

- By age two there is already a wide difference between children's sleeping patterns. Some children will sleep 12 hours straight through the night, while others may sleep as few as seven hours plus their daytime nap. The easiest way to tell if your child is getting enough sleep is by assessing how awake and alert they are during the day.

29TH NOVEMBER

I'm panicking. My chest is crushed by an invisible weight, and the tears behind my eyes could quench a volcano. And all this because I've been watching a PG rated TV series in which a little boy just got carried off by a monster, in front of his mother's screaming face. It's only a story, and my better half is already concocting stories whereby the little boy is obviously saved off screen. I feel like a fool. I know there aren't any monsters living locally. But there are people. There are people, there are wars, conflict, irrational acts of violence, cars and buses; a thousand and one things ready to snatch my little boy from me. How can I protect my son from the world?

I feel like King Canute trying to turn back not a watery tide, but a flood of danger. All life is risk. I know that pointless fear can poison life, but I am so damned scared that I will not always be able to protect my baby. He trusts me to make his world safe. He has yet to learn Mama is not an all powerful being.

Why don't these fonging film writers think about the effect of their light entertainment on mothers of young children?

BEING AFRAID

As the parent of a small child you will often be afraid. I suspect that fear continues throughout your child's life, but right now when their common sense is in inverse proportion to their mobility and curiosity, there are so many good reasons to be afraid. Every day we have to find a balance between caution and unreasonable fear. Every day we have to accept that sometimes bad things can happen no matter what precautions we take. We need to encourage our children to be brave, but not stupidly fearless. Every day is a challenge.

30TH NOVEMBER

Right, almost got Christmas sorted. A giant easel for 3+ (which I only noticed after I had bought it), a free tub of drawing type things (I shall have to watch in case he swallows any) and all the stuff I'd got already. Incredibly annoyed with the store, which claims to be the greatest toyshop in Britain and which, only after I'd rung them three times, deigned to tell me my 48 hour delivery hadn't happened because there were 128 back orders on the bearchair I'd chosen, and the last stock order was in October (for 12), which still hadn't arrived. I ended up cancelling my order.

4TH DECEMBER

I believe on a psychic level the Emperor knows the famous toy store has let us down and is angry. Surely, only this could explain his sudden desire to throw his toys around the room. We're not talking about the fabulous flights of Stinky Bear here. We're talking large, plastic constructions with lights and flashing buttons and gismos and stuff. The kind of thing when you're pregnant you swear you will never buy, until your child explains quite clearly that wooden toys are for parents and they want things that go buzz.

Things that go buzz are quite weighty, so I'm trying to convince the Emperor that if I take him up or down the stairs against his will, my being smacked in the side of the head with one is sore.

Everyone says, don't carry him, make him walk – but at two and a little bit, the Emperor has discovered the skill of turning his body to jelly. There's a small hand in mine, my long fingers wrapped around his wrist, and the rest of him is this slack, drooping form, that will only move if I drag him – and I'm terrified that if I drag him something will pop out of its socket. He's like one of those little wooden toys I had as a kid, which when you pressed a button on the underside lost all their tautness and went utterly limp. It's making going for a walk, in fact doing any of those outing things Mamas and Emperors are meant to do, very difficult. My mother tells me her GP says boys are more difficult than girls.

Yeah, right. People with boys have it easy. I have an Emperor.

THE IMMOVABLE TODDLER

Sometimes for no good reason your toddler will refuse to go where you want them to go. During this year, this is liable to become a frequent occurrence. Think ahead. If you only have a short time to nip out to do something then seriously consider postponing or working around the errand. If you cannot, take a buggy. Let the child push it if they do not wish to ride. It's a useful back up when you need to start putting on the speed.

If you're with a walking toddler, inside or out, then you have to take your time unless you are strong and fearless enough to pick up an unhappy child. Never drag a child by the arm; it simply isn't safe. Be prepared that if you are insistent on going somewhere your toddler does not wish to go (like away from the play park) that they are likely to throw themselves to the ground, wail and refuse to move. Other parents seeing this will understand; everyone else will look at you as if you are a child beater.

Chill; remember you are the adult, and that in the scale of things almost everything can wait. **Life with a toddler is slower.**

Keep promises about returning to play parks, doing things later and nice things that will happen once they start moving again. Forewarn a child when you need to leave, for example that after one more slide you have to go and keep to the plan. Explain, reason and be consistent in your intentions. Be strong, wait for the storm to pass and keep on doing what you said you were going to do. It's the only way for a toddler to understand boundaries. Use picking a child up as a last resort. Sometimes you will need to do this to keep them safe, but if you can avoid hauling them away do so. Ideally you want your child to understand that there are times you both need to go places, and encourage them to work with you rather than against you.

5TH DECEMBER

The contents of the Emperor's nappy this morning resembled a medium sized green gerbil. The little paper seams were sagging at the edges. If it weren't Christmas soon, I'd be trying for potty training. Unless, of course, I could get the rest of the family to potty train him for me?

TOILET TRAINING: KNOWING WHEN TO BEGIN

Don't make a drama out of a crisis. Children will display interest in their bodily functions. Be firm, but not openly horrified, about what is acceptable and what is not.

- Toilet training can only work when a child is aware of their bladder and bowel movements. This usually happens any time between 18 months and three years.

- Children need to be able to rearrange their own clothes, and to understand and follow simple instructions.

- Children indicate this awareness in a variety of ways: pointing at a full nappy or squatting in a corner and grunting when passing a bowel movement. When they are reasonably consistent in this behaviour, you can start potty training (of which more later).

It is important to pick a time when the household has the minimum of upheavals and there is no particular stress on the child. Summertime is especially good – fewer layers of clothes to deal with.

6ᵀᴴ DECEMBER

The kitchen door has had a pedicure, and a bolt has been affixed two thirds of the way up. All poisonous products have been removed from the downstairs toilet, and the Emperor has suddenly lost all interest in trying to open his gate.

TODDLER PROOFING

Remember when you baby proofed everything? This year there will be an increasing number of safety concerns as your toddler becomes more and more mobile. You still need to check that all those plug sockets are covered, but you also need to check that even the higher windows are now locked.

Toddlers climb. They use chairs. They stack toys. Many of those things that were safely out of reach like medicine cabinets are no longer inaccessible. All medicines and inedible substances need to be securely locked away. (And yes, this does include open bags of cat food.) However, please resist the temptation simply to move things to higher shelves. This has two effects: it makes furniture unstable and keeps the banished (and therefore desirable object) within sight. Every year children die because they pull furniture down on top of themselves, or because they scale chairs and tables to reach open windows. Two year olds have even been known to hang themselves from curtain cords.

Your home is not a death trap, but you do need to assess risks. There will always be areas that are unsafe. My kitchen is so tiny I decided not simply to lock the cupboard under the sink where all the nasty things are kept, but to lock the door. It was going to be all too easy for him to help himself to knives from drawers, turn on the gas taps or stick his tongue to the inside of the freezer.

- Any room where your child plays for any time without supervision needs low furniture, no hanging cords or leads, no exposed plugs, no windows that little fingers can open and no poisonous or inedible substances.

- I know you're not going be leaving them in the house alone, but it only takes moments for a child to get into danger. Really, when you think about it, it's surprising any of us made it to adulthood.

- The desire to explore comes along with increased mobility and an almost complete absence of common sense. Remember toddlers have no fear; they give it to their parents to hold. Each home will have its own unique style of risks, and no one can possibly tell you them all. The only way to get an idea is to get down to roughly the right size and take a fresh and exhaustive look at each and every room.

- Imagine yourself two and a bit feet tall, then scramble round on your knees seeing where you can stick your fingers and how many things you can pick up and put in your mouth.

- Then check for spaces and gaps that are toddler sized, and make them safe. For your own peace of mind do something about the cat litter tray and its tempting contents of long, tubular, chocolate shaped things.

9TH DECEMBER

Christmas shopping and the unpleasant discovery that posh stores don't cater for buggies. We're trying to get to the big tree with the hundreds of little red lights in the middle of the shop. Everywhere there are stairs. I end up popping in and out of lifts like some demented jack-in-the-box, until finally I give in and allow my companion to carry the Emperor down to the Christmas lights. By this time I'm too frazzled, sweaty and irritable to go myself. My son does me proud. He points at the tree. Says "Tree" a few times and then "Mama ,where –r-ooo?" before pelting back across the shop floor, scattering the contents of the lower shelves in his little wake, to the safety of his buggy. Serves them right. Obviously, this is the kind of place where they expect shoppers to leave their children outside with the nanny.

Finally have all the Emperor's presents, and most of everyone else's. However, I have no Christmas decorations up, no cards written and my holiday is littered with half-formed plans – not least of which is my intention to take advantage of everyone being home, and ask them to entertain his Imperialness while I work.

12TH DECEMBER

Found out today White Ladder Press is taking this diary. They tried to tell me two days ago, but the Emperor had hidden both phone handsets, which had subsequently lost power and been unable to offer even the tiniest peep. His phone obsession is getting out of control.

THE FESTIVE SEASON

Unless there are remarkable grandparents, last year you will have experienced the serial indulgence issue, where each parent takes a turn to be merry. This year, not only sobriety but extra alertness is needed around your extremely active toddler, who will doubtless try to climb the Christmas tree, eat the cracker snaps and pop the fairy lights. This year decorations need to be sturdy and out of snatching reach.

- The festive feast poses more problems. Some toddler parents opt to invite everyone round instead of travelling back and forth between in-laws and friends. I think this is fine if you're prepared to hire a caterer (and let's face it this isn't on the agenda for most of us). Otherwise you are going to be the one

---

running around tidying, cooking, hosting and, above all, missing a lot of your toddler's delight in Christmas.

- Just as importantly your toddler is going to be missing you. Doting relatives showering presents are fun for a while, but Mum and Dad are what make the world go round. Be wary of overloading the day.

- It really is fine to keep Christmas to yourself – your baby is only two once, and goodness knows you deserve to enjoy the good bits.

- If people must come round, then they need to contribute. We're not talking the odd cup of tea here, or bottle of wine: get them to bring a dish.

- Alternatively, and this is my favourite option, arrange to meet people over the three week period. (The Emperor loves outings.) But add the caveat if the weather is bad or the toddler worn out then the day will have to be postponed.

- It's your baby, be selfish and enjoy the holidays.

14TH DECEMBER

Huge argument with Dada over the issue of smacking. The Emperor was having a naughty day – and unless you've experienced the scope of Imperial naughtiness you have experienced nothing. The Emperor's father eventually decided that he was being too naughty and was probably over tired and needed to go to bed. In reply the Emperor picked up a wooden mask and banged it off a glass door. Dada planted a brisk, but not hard, smack on the base of the nappy and sternly told the Emperor it was bedtime now. With hindsight I doubt the Emperor even felt the tap through the padding of his nappy, but at the time I leapt out of my seat to rescue my poor baby, completely undermining his father's authority, and demanded the screaming and crying Emperor be cuddled and shown he is still loved. (He is, I later realise, screaming and crying because he didn't manage to break the glass.)

His exasperated father at this point gives the Emperor into my care, and after a chase around the house I get him into bed, read him his story and he falls straight asleep. (He was extremely tired.)

Then I go back to confront his father on the issue of smacking.

SMACKING

Between the two of us we represent the most popular views on physical punishment.

Dada believes that sometimes a wilful child, especially one with limited communication skills, needs a tap on the bottom to pull him into line – and the gods only know the Emperor is a wilful child. In particular, his father believes it is important to hold this in reserve if the child is endangering themselves, for example attempting to break glass or throw themselves off a railway platform.

I believe that smacking a child frightens them, makes them more liable to disobey and rebel, and sets an example that physical retaliation is acceptable.

Neither of us believes it is in any way conscionable to smack a child hard enough to leave the slightest mark. Nor does either of us accept that more than one sharp tap is acceptable. The law in England and Wales now explicitly allows for reasonable chastisement in the form of a mild smack that leaves no mark. To be honest this new regulation seems to confuse more than help most parents. It's probably easiest to think that deliberately causing actual physical, mental or emotional harm to a child is liable to get you prosecuted anywhere in the UK. A tap to reinforce a point will not.

Whatever path you decide to follow the essential core is that punishment is consistent. Otherwise you cause the child distress and confusion without teaching anything. Teaching a child that violence is a superior argument ('If you do that I'll smack you, so don't do it') can create an adolescent who believes that with the power of might they can get their own way.

But a child who has no respect for discipline will only listen to their own desires, and is unlikely to socialise well.

Toddlers can drive you to the edge of sanity, and a punishment administered in rage is always wrong. You need to be clear about how you discipline, so when a situation occurs you deal with it rationally no matter how tired or frazzled you feel. Lashing out in anger will always cause mental and emotional damage if not physical damage, and to both of you. Our children are biologically programmed to love us unconditionally for the first few years of life. After that we have to earn their love and respect by being the best parents we can be.

18TH DECEMBER

It's good that the Emperor is saying, "Santa" and "Cwiswmas twee". He needs the cute points.

In my topsy-turvy house I needed to take him downstairs to

change a thoroughly obnoxious nappy, only two stone of lashing, struggling, furious toddler did not want to go. I know he was fretting because he was due his afternoon nap (I'm trying to get the routine back on track), but this was harder than shopping on Christmas Eve. In the bedroom there was total refusal to get on the changing mat. I should be starting toilet training, but Christmas seems such the wrong time to do this.

WHAT ARE TANTRUMS?

Frustration.

At two a toddler is becoming much more aware. The world is very big and they are very little. Toddlers need enormous courage and determination to struggle through all the growing challenges ahead. Fortunately, they have a natural, inbuilt drive to succeed. Unfortunately, they don't yet have any sense of when it is appropriate to use this drive. They may desperately want to climb over the fireguard and into the fire, but as a responsible parent you will have to stop them setting the house and themselves on fire. The result is often a tantrum. Similarly they may know that the round peg goes in the round hole, but be unable to co-ordinate well enough to finish the puzzle. The result? A toy thrown across the room, tears and screaming.

Tantrums are scary for both parents and children. The toddler is in the grip of strong emotions they can't control and which are completely overwhelming.

Parents can find them overwhelming too.

- No matter how calm and excellent a parent you are, your toddler will have tantrums.

- Toddlers don't want to have tantrums any more than parents want to deal with them. Having a tantrum isn't being 'naughty';

a tantrum is about learning to control anger and frustration, and this takes time.

- Try to anticipate your child's triggers.

- Many tantrums are avoidable. Hunger, frustration, tiredness and illness all make tantrums more likely. Anticipating the need for snacks and naps helps, as does spotting potentially frustrating situations such as completing a difficult task. (You can intervene and help the child solve the situation before the frustration level hits the point of no return.)

- Not wishing to do something can bring on a terrible rage. If a particular issue always causes a tantrum ask yourself if it is necessary. However, once you've begun do not change your behaviour or you will reinforce the message that tantrums work.

- If the tantrum is often triggered by a necessary event (like bedtime), give a warning beforehand (10 minutes to bedtime). If the tantrum starts allow it to go for two or three minutes before physically moving the child to where they need to be. Talk about what is happening with them and try to distract them before the tantrum gets into swing.

- Talking and helping your child talk about what is making them angry will help them manage their feelings. It is difficult for toddlers to verbalise their feelings, and practice helps them do this. However, do not interrogate the child, and do not ask them to provide explanations for behaviour you cannot explain yourself. This will only lead to fright and confusion.

- Never become visibly upset yourself.

- If the tantrum is in a public place, move the child to as quiet a space as you can find.

- If a toddler is totally out of control consider holding them firmly for one to three minutes. Children vary, but some may be frightened by their loss of emotional control and find this immensely comforting.

GENERAL RULE: once a tantrum starts give the child time to calm down in a quiet space; their bedroom or a playpen. Tell them why you are doing this, and go back and talk with them in five minutes. (A minute is a very long time when you're a toddler). Repeat as necessary.

21ST DECEMBER

The Emperor's language is taking off. He copies words regularly, and occasionally he comes out with phrases that mean he does understand like "TV duck. The duck is TV duck", which is obviously a reference to that fat yellow character.

But today at the museum he excelled himself, choosing the Sex Pistols track in the retro room, and chanting, "I am the anti-Christ", before throwing himself onto the floor for a serious laughing fit. He also enjoyed yelling "destroy". Should I worry?

24TH DECEMBER

A Christmas Story

Once there was a mother who was trying to be very organised in November. She ordered toys for her son for Christmas from the toymaker. Sadly, in conference with the elves over that month, it became increasingly clear that they could not deliver, and she cancelled the greater part of the order. Meanwhile the Emperor read the old catalogue, and spent many hours looking at the page that showed the picture of what his mother had wanted to buy him.

Then on Christmas Eve, the postman came bearing an enormous box, and the Emperor squealed in joy; the cancelling of orders was nothing compared to his Imperial will.

Sadly, his mother's credit card was still charged.

29TH DECEMBER

Ian, who has an avowed dislike of children, yet always plays with the Emperor, commented on my son's tendency to point rather than ask for things; James, his nephew, is not allowed to point. Suddenly I'm back at his sister's wedding last year when his lawyer brother, whose son is slightly older than the Emperor, sat me down seriously to ask if I allowed pointing. I didn't have a clue what he was talking about. I'm now logging this as something they teach you at nursery (and I mean teach the parents). How on earth was I to know that the Emperor's cute habit of pointing at objects of desire and frowning, as if he was trying to use some telekinetic force to bring them to him, would make him extremely lazy with his vocabulary? But it does. Pointing is bad or at least unhelpful. I am a bad Mama. The Emperor can say many words, but most of the time he refuses to utter them, preferring instead to command through increasing threatening Imperial gestures.

LANGUAGE

You are going to hear this mantra throughout the book: children progress at their own rate. Roughly, during this year you can expect your two year old to go from three word sentences to six or seven word sentences that demonstrate not only an understanding of words, but allow them to frame questions and argue. It is a year of massive language change. In particular I found that once my son started mixing with other children he began to speak in sentences. It seems he could already do so, but it simply wasn't necessary around family, who understood his every need.

- Speak directly to your toddler, and leave time for them to respond. Toddlers take far longer than adults to process meaning in sentences.

- Don't be tempted to finish their sentences for them.

- Reading and singing helps facilitate language acquisition – that's why nursery rhymes are so appealing to children.

- Introduce new words in context.

5TH JANUARY

New Year passed quietly, not least because everyone had caught this January's new virus, and Dada has proved his worth. For the last few nights, above and beyond the call of duty, Dada dealt with a little boy with a blocked nose, who every time he settled down to sleep, made a terrible discovery; he couldn't suck his thumb and breathe. The wailing and lamentations echoed from shore to shore but I slept through, and thus have a chance of making some of my other deadlines.

Then, this afternoon at 2pm, the Emperor started wheezing. I had terrible breathing problems as a child, and my BMA flow chart self-help book is quite clear that wheezing is a take your child to the doctor now situation.

I phone the receptionist and pull the never fails "I know there's probably nothing wrong, but he's only two" line and sure enough I get the "Don't worry, love, I'd be the same." And we're in for a five minute appointment at the end of the day.

USE THE NATIONAL HEALTH

If you're worried about your child's health, see a doctor. If you feel you are being unreasonably concerned over your child's health, see a doctor yourself. Children are remarkably robust, but there are danger signs you can't ignore. The Children's Medical Guide by the British Medical Association, published by DK, is very helpful but nothing can replace a visit to your local GP. If in doubt, visit the NHS Direct website at **www.nhsdirect.nhs.uk**, which provides a lot of information on general issues or, in more urgent cases, call NHS Direct who will advise you if you need to see a GP. The number for England and Wales is 0845 46 47, and for Scotland 08454 24 24 24 (the service is not currently available in Northern Ireland).

5TH JANUARY (eve)

The verdict: the Emperor has croup. Whenever he's upset or active he starts barking like a small puppy. By the time his name was called at the very busy surgery tonight he was growling like a little rottweiler: another parent had encouraged her child to share her toy. Unfortunately, the Emperor doesn't understand sharing yet, and hates giving things back. However, it did give the bright 'n' cheerful GP a chance to hear some intense wheezing.

Tonight is likely to be bad too and, if he's like the majority of small children, he will be fully recovered in the next couple of days. A small percentage, the GP tells me, get so inflamed that they need further treatment, and tells me to call the surgery day or night if he gets worse. I did the right thing in taking him to the GP (brownie point). The best thing I can do for the Emperor is keep him calm, and apologise endlessly for inflicting this evil upon him. Croup, although it only occurs in infants, is a side effect of the cold virus. (Minus several million brownie points for infecting him in the first place.)

9TH JANUARY

We're well into the New Year and it feels as if nothing has changed. Rationally, I know this will be a year of great developments for the Emperor, but his Imperial Highness seems much as he ever did.

It doesn't matter how much time I spend sitting in front of the new pretty alphabet spinner, saying "Show me duck" or doing whatever the latest 'how to encourage your child' book has told me to do, he does not perform for me: he needs his audience.

I used to feel I was totally out of sync with him, that I was a bad mother, but truth is simple: I am furniture. I am the wallpaper on his monitor of life. Mama is always here. New people, even Dada who isn't here all day, are citizens of his little empire that he needs to win over again and again, and like an Imperial diplomat he brings out all the charm and all his learning to play to the crowd. It's hard not to feel unappreciated.

Every day we continue our struggles with food. He will now only eat things that are sweet, crunchy and non-vegetable. It's not unusual, but it is trying. I have tried the nastiest approach I can think of: not giving him anything on his plate but that which I want him to try. Nothing happens. The Emperor would rather starve than eat things he doesn't recognise. He's also started feeding me a small piece of his food before he will eat any. I can't help but feel like the Imperial poison taster, very disposable.

And then there's the spitting. Of all the problems toddlers can develop, like head banging or breath holding, spitting must be the most embarrassing for parents. My father in tones of strict disapproval asked where he picked up such a habit while I, feeling like a chastised teenager again, hasten to reassure him none of my friends spit.

BAD HABITS

Most bad habits are severe tantrums. They are about pushing boundaries and, of course, also about seeking attention. If like me you do actually have duties other than pandering to your Emperor or Empress's needs (going to the loo or making lunch being included here) then there will be times when you can't play when they want, and they will let you know they're displeased. Now, psychologists will tell you that toddlers and babies love boundaries as much as they like to push them. They are not little starship captains going where no baby has gone before for the hell of it. They are trying to establish the perimeters of their world. And you and I know, as parents, that is not what it feels like.

So here's a basic reassuring low-down one parent to another.

Breath holding

Your child cannot harm themselves by deliberately holding their breath; that clever hindbrain kicks in and starts them breathing the moment they pass out. However, sometimes you can distract the child from holding their breath. Toddlers can hurt themselves when they fall. The trick is to be ready to catch the child if they pass out, and then dart out of the room, but be near enough to listen to make sure all is well. If your toddler believes they will get extra attention for this behaviour it will continue. Be aware that breath holding can bring on jerking, seizure type motions.

Rarely, however, passing out after appearing to hold the breath can be the sign of something more serious. The first time your child pulls this particular brand of tantrum you should have them checked out by your doctor to rule out any more serious cause. Also the time they are passed out should be very short; seconds not minutes.

Head-banging

Some younger children do this because they like the noise. (I had to put cardboard over the ends of the Emperor's bed for a while when he was younger.) If your child is using head-banging to act up – ie dropping to the floor and banging their head once or twice in a tantrum – then apart from the times when you feel you need to remove them for safety's sake (for example if they try this on a concrete floor), then you can treat this like any other tantrum and not respond. Rushing over to rescue them will generally encourage your toddler to do this again whenever they want your attention.

However repeated head-banging, where a child sits alone and does this constantly, can be a warning sign of emotional or psychological imbalance. If you suspect it is about the noise they are making, then using cardboard or cushions to prevent the sound should stop the habit. If it doesn't, see your doctor.

Spitting

As this is yet to be cured with the Emperor I can only tell you what I'm doing and hope it works. Spitting is rewarded with a time-out in the playpen and/or removal of a toy – although I can never bring myself to take away Stinky Bear.

Hair pulling

Some children pull out their own hair from frustration or anxiety. If this is excessive then it is a good idea to see your doctor.

Biting and hitting

In some children violence is a first line response to annoyance. Don't take it personally. Answer such episodes with time-outs.

The general answer: sometimes these behaviours can be the sign something is wrong. In particular if any of the above is happening more than five times a day; there are other behavioural problems; development appears delayed or your child is injuring themselves, then it's time to see a doctor.

Any and all bad habits will persist if the toddler perceives he or she is gaining from this. Sometimes physically containing a child, as with a tantrum, can help. A calm, measured response of a time-out is generally an effective weapon. Most bad habits should fade by four or five years old.

10TH JANUARY

I'm at a party and trying hard not to think about the Emperor. I discover two things. Firstly, I have a higher requirement for parties than BE (Before Emperor). I have so much less time for people whom I don't find interesting, or whom I consider dull. I used to be more tolerant than this, but if I'm giving up playing Kiss-Kiss or Where's My Nose, you've got to show me some decent entertainment. I do often feel isolated or trapped at home, but when I'm back out in the wild, wild world I used to find so much fun, very often it isn't.

But secondly, I did learn from one lady, a lawyer with three girls, how important the movie 'Billy Elliot' is. Someone crassly introduced us to each other as "you're both mothers you'll get along". I was so shocked I didn't even kick him. Strangely enough we both obediently fell into talking about our children, and I told the story of the Emperor learning some very unfortunate words. She explained that this too happened to her. She'd been doing very well until her washing machine broke, then on one day the children learnt a whole new subsection to their vocabulary. Her children are older (8+) now, and they have an agreement: they can swear inside the house if they must but never outside. But if they forget this rule, she blames it on them watching 'Billy Elliot' I tell her of this book, and how it will be largely full of my mistakes. "But you can do that now," she says, "admit we make mistakes. Not so long ago we all had to be perfect mothers. Now it's OK not to get everything right."

13TH JANUARY

Wee small hours of the morning. I foolishly wrote that the Emperor was not changing or moving on, and now he has acquired three new habits. The first, a new game of Big Hug followed by a pat on my back and a small cry of 'aww!', is very appealing. This is just as well. Yet again he needs all the cute points he can get. The spitting is getting out of hand, a range of at least six feet and continuous when he is upset. (I didn't know babies had so much spit in them.) But his shiny second habit, in ascending scale of awfulness is that he now throws all food he doesn't recognise on the floor without tasting it. He will no longer eat rice or any of the other savoury food he used to like. It's bread, biscuits, potatoes (crispy), chocolate or ice cream. I know this is a terrible, terrible diet, but he simply will not eat anything else. He'll cry from hunger and still not touch the awful food I bestow upon him.

But the final new habit, the one that breaks me into tiny pieces: suddenly he no longer wants to be left on his own for even five minutes. During the day this is difficult, but at night getting him to sleep is impossible. We're so tired that Dada is doing what we know is only a quick fix solution by climbing into bed with him until he falls asleep. He's not even napping in the afternoon. From being a self-assured, confident and independent toddler, he's suddenly become clingier than your average roll of sticky tape. I can only assume he's traumatised by the sudden lack of presents after his November and December fests. I've been working through the textbook causes of disruption of sleep patterns in my head – arguments, disturbances and the like, and all I can come up with is that he slept badly when he had croup. Is he afraid on some level if he falls asleep he will wake up wheezing and coughing? Am I being too fanciful? But if I'm right how do I explain to a two year old it's all alright without one of us climbing into bed and hugging him?

15TH JANUARY

For the second night ever I am away from the Emperor, thanks to a special deal at a conference hotel touting for business. It's a huge, empty Marie Celeste of a place and my corridor (where I am the only occupant) looks like a set from Alice in

Wonderland with crazy patterned carpet that echoes endlessly in huge mirrors.

After a nice dinner accompanied by an excellent red (I haven't drunk this much wine in sooo long; not feeling I am able to be inebriated whilst in charge of a toddler) I drink decaf coffee in the totally empty cocktail lounge, and try to peer out of the window into the night to see the local hills and mountains.

I am so tired, and my perspective is returning. I am beginning to remember what it was like to be me, alone. I know the Emperor is safe with his Dada (and I have only phoned once) and I am unwinding beyond what I thought was possible. When I'm around the Emperor it doesn't matter who else is looking after him, even his Dada or his Goddad, I can't help watching 24-7. (He's not a quiet and calm child.) It's not that I don't trust his Dada, or anyone else; it's that I can't switch off. This is a bad thing – and it's only when I stop I realise how fraught I generally am.

I struggle to sleep. In the end I do drift off for a while, but guess what? I'm missing the buzz of the monitor (which normally drives me up the wall) but through which I listen to the Emperor sleep.

When I get home I am greeted by a happy, smiley little face which pronounces perfectly, "Hallo Mama". The Emperor, it seems, is a perfectly content child who is psychologically speaking so well adjusted that he perfectly trusts his mother will come back; the clingy child of yesterday is gone. He is also speaking close to RP (received pronunciation or BBC-speak), which is doubtless going to get him into as much trouble in the playground as it did me.

Home, this morning, I am so very tired I ask the Emperor to

spend a couple of hours in the safety zone and finally fall
asleep to the sound of him playing, and seeing how far he can
spit.

17ᵀᴴ JANUARY

My son ate his first piece of orange today – chocolate orange.
Will the Emperor ever eat real food?

20ᵀᴴ JANUARY

The cats have their revenge. One of them (possibly both)
climbed into the Emperor's toy chest and peed on his stuffed
toy animals (aka stuffies). Fortunately Stinky Bear was not
there. Nevertheless the Emperor is demanding severe and
bloody punishments. Thankfully the Fimble survived his wash,
or there would have been two episodes of caticide.

PETS AND CHILDREN

Cats and dogs may tolerate new babies, with varying degrees of
enthusiasm, but once a child starts toddling around not only has
their owner's attention diminished radically, but their territory is
being invaded.

- It's vitally important that pets have an area they can retreat to
  away from the child. Also, you will need to supervise your
  child's interaction with the animals. Children don't understand
  that it isn't funny if the cat shrieks when they pull its tail.

- The likelihood is that cats will scratch and dogs will retreat or
  even growl until your child learns to behave properly.
  However, at the beginning you need to be on your guard in

---

case your pet is one of the rare ones that will not tolerate children. In which case you will need to rehome. (Do also remember to de-flea and regularly worm all pets that so require.)

Generally, much loved family pets do tolerate children, and toddlers will usually follow your lead and treat your animals with respect. Showing your animal affection, and encouraging your child to pet them at the same time, goes a long way to cementing pet-child relations.

21ST JANUARY

Today the Emperor's father noticed he was somewhat consonantly challenged – in particular with l's. His repeated pronunciation of a favourite new word 'clock' is causing us all embarrassment.

24TH JANUARY

On Thursday I had a truly wonderful day with the Emperor. He was cuddly, affectionate, didn't spit at anything, and was the sweetest little boy in the world. The following day he was back to his tricks of throwing things at the cats, spitting, eating chalk and stropping. It's taken me until today (Saturday) to figure out what was going wrong.

On Tuesday and Wednesday I had been unreasonably busy. The Emperor and I did have our play sessions. He did get fed and changed but, honestly, it was a case of less rather than more. For a lot of the day he was required to play with his toys on his own. As he is a very imaginative child, this isn't too much of a hardship – and I always sop my conscience with the thought that at least we are in the same room – at least I'm there. When Thursday came along, and the business abated, I decided to make it up to the poor little chap, and dedicated the day to him.

28ᵀᴴ JANUARY

The Emperor persists in persecuting the cats. He screams at them, and spits into their fur. He likes to make them react. He can't understand (and is probably at this stage incapable of it) that they are living creatures that deserve respect. My older cat, who has been with me for 15 years, is pulling all her fur out in distress. Andrew, a friend of mine, round for coffee one evening, says he remembers his little brother behaving the same way when he was little. I asked what happened. "The cat left home," he answers.

5ᵀᴴ FEBRUARY

I'm back to thinking about speech. I've been reading around the Internet on the number of words a child should have by his age, and the results are startlingly different. I've determined I am going to try and keep a list of the words he says over the next few days. Today we had 'Teddy bear', 'Clifford', 'Douglas', 'Mama, juice now!', 'Up', 'Downstairs', 'Rusk', 'Chocolate now!' 'Big hug!' 'Cuppa tea', 'Mama's tea', 'Butterfly', 'Cat', 'Cats', 'Flowers', 'Car', 'Dinosaur', 'Horse', 'Hand', 'Hands', 'One, two, three, four, five, six, seven, eight, nine, ten, yay!', 'clap', 'tasty', 'duck', and 'bath'.

Is it cheating to count plurals?

VOCABULARY

Keeping lists does help. It can demonstrate patterns of interest your child is following or things they are missing. Recording the words they speak can put at rest your fears they are falling behind, or if you still feel your child is behind, it gives you something to show your health visitor or GP. Slow speech development can be due to physical problems (like hearing, or palate deformities), emotional difficulties (a difficult atmosphere at home), or be down to your child being the strong and silent type. It is rarely the sign of anything serious, but as I've said elsewhere, if you're worried make a nuisance of yourself at the doctors: it's what they're paid for.

10TH FEBRUARY

At the weekend he had a minor strop in the toy store while being wheeled in the trolley. For this read: he stood up, screamed and refused to sit down again – and all because he couldn't have some TV related toy from a show he doesn't even watch. But I finally feel I am getting a handle on these temper tantrums. We no longer bring shopping malls to a standstill. He turns a few heads, but I think we are both coming to terms with his red faced, vein popping rages. His frustration with the world is calming and so am I. And now, into all of this, I have to bring the toilet monster. He can pull his pants both up and down. This is really the last hurdle. I'm beginning to have nightmares of what he may do in shops shortly.

TV SHOWS, VIOLENCE AND ETHICAL TOYS

By the time toddlers are 23 months they are information glut-tons, repeating words and actions incessantly. This brings all kinds of problems from gender stereotyping to copying behav-iour. No one would deny children model their behaviour on the people around them; television is more difficult. Endless rounds of experiments by psychologists have proved first one thing and then another – as a psychologist myself, I can see how that can be. But it doesn't matter what modern science says about the influence of the one eyed living room monster, it is what you notice in your child and what you feel comfortable with. Children do copy what they see. They learn through mimicking and role playing. However, this is done without understanding. They will need to be a fair few years older before they appreciate the pain another child feels is the same as the pain they would feel in iden-tical circumstances.

I don't want to bring up my child to believe the world is a fairytale place of goodness and love because it isn't, and sadly he will need to know this to survive. However, I need him to understand while there is love and security at home, actions always have consequences and when people are hurt they stay hurt.

- Child healthcare experts recommend limiting TV to two hours a day, with anything over four hours being considered exces-sive.

- Evidence suggests most children will not become more vio-lent from watching TV violence (unless there are already other problems). However they may become overly fearful for their own safety, less sympathetic to real victims of violence, peri-ods of aggressive play may increase, and in extreme cases (from watching a violent over 18 movie) can develop some-thing similar to post traumatic stress disorder.

- The best advice is to watch specific shows rather than have the TV on as a background activity, and to turn the telly off once this is over.

- While it's not healthy for a toddler to be aggressive (in terms of deliberately harming other children) it is normal and healthy to incorporate aggressive behaviour into play, and this tends to happen regardless of whether children are allowed toy soldiers or toy guns. Boys do this to a larger extent than girls.

- With increased fears of violence some parents may choose to disallow realistic toy weapons in case these are confused with the real thing (as has unfortunately happened in the USA on rare occasions).

REVIEW: A QUARTER OF THE WAY THROUGH THE TERRIBLE TWOS

MY GOALS

1 By the time he is three the Emperor will be eating a healthy mixed diet without complaint, and pudding bribes will be a thing of the past.

I'm going to give us a 6/10 for this not because he is eating everything I'd like to him eat or because he has ever knowingly swallowed a vegetable, but because we are doing well enough. He is healthy.

2 Nappies will be a dim memory, with all bodily waste products going in the loo, without having to go through the hell of pottydom.

This is on my mind a lot, but apart from occasionally showing some awareness of his bodily functions the Emperor and I get a 2/10 here.

3   Every night the Emperor will go down for at least 10 hours of undisturbed rest.

He frequently sleeps up to 12 hours. However, points knocked off for very irregular bedtimes. 7/10

4   As mother I will continually strive to provide entertainment and activities suitable for the Emperor's developing mind and body (which includes ethically correct selection of toys and television programs).

I'm proud of my choices here. Except he keeps being given flashing, noisy things that don't exactly encourage active play. The kind of thing that after pushing a button expects a toddler to do nothing but sit back in awe. Thank goodness for his reverse engineering skills. 7/10

5   I will begin the socialisation process of the Emperor by finding him other children to play with, and cease surrounding him totally with servile adults.

Total failure. I haven't found him anyone to play with and all my friends and family abide by his slightest whim. 0/10

6   At the end of the year, the Emperor will be able to give his real name and address when asked, and will be fluent in conversational adult-speak.

It's not an easy street name to say. He can say the street and the house number, but not much more. 3/10

7   I will ensure that the Emperor's surroundings are safe, and that we never have another occurrence of the collapsed babygate and the stairs.

See me here clinging onto a large piece of wood for luck. So far, apart from your normal bumps and bruises occasioned by running into the world too fast, he's doing fine. 10/10

8   I will undertake to school the Emperor in the ways of acceptable behaviour without resorting to corporal punishment, or anything that may entail long term therapy (for either of us) at a later date.

I'm not sure I won't need long term therapy, but he's fine. It's just a pity about his behaviour. 5/10

9   I will not work full time. I will devote huge amounts of each day to the caring of the Emperor and his environs, but I will also write, study and achieve a minimal level of social life.

I'm still writing part time and giving him plenty of attention. However my social life is reaching the terminal stage. 6/10

10 I will not be a sucker for the Emperor's huge blue topaz eyes or other formidable weapons in his armoury of manipulation and cajolement.

As if. 4/10

THE EMPEROR'S GOAL

1   To bend the known universe to his will.

6/10 (He's winning. Need I say more?)

17TH FEBRUARY

Major landmark on two fronts today. The Emperor finally scaled the side of his playpen to ultimate freedom. The bedroom gate is going to be next. But more importantly we went for a walk.

This doesn't sound like much, but when you bear in mind we never use his tricycle alone because I know I'll be left holding the trike while he scampers off into the distance, you might begin to understand.

23RD FEBRUARY

I have to start potty training. I have to. The poos are getting so big the last one was down to his knees.

And food – after all the carefully prepared meals he's wasted, today's lumps of carbonised bread with blobs of half melted cheese were greeted with a cry of "Yum! Yum! Tasty!" He also says this when he's eating the bubbles in his bath, so I didn't make too much of it. Half an hour later he's still eating (the cheese not the bubbles).

BEING THE BEST MUM

I daily berate myself for not doing enough: for not managing to convince the Emperor that carrots are fun and yum, yum, tasty; for not toilet training him by 18 months; for discovering he learns more words from cbeebies than from me; for never playing with him enough; for not teaching him brain surgery and all the rest. In fact, I'm very good at ruining all my time with him by worrying I'm not only not doing it right, I'm also not doing enough.

I've spoken to a number of other parents, new and experienced, and these feelings are remarkably common.

When you think about it, what bigger responsibility will any of us ever have, than being entrusted with a new and vulnerable life. No wonder none of us feels up to it.

The closest I ever came to this feeling before was working as a counsellor, and having clients hand me their broken, fragile lives

---

and expect me to stick them back together. Of course I couldn't. They did the work, but I could be there for them.

Sometimes it seems being a mother is much the same. Toddlers learn at their own rate, eat (it seems) whatever they decide they need, and even choose when they can control their own bodies when it comes to toilet training.

What we do as parents is primarily to provide a safe environment and to be there. On occasion we will be invited in on the playing, but as we move through the twos, your tiny baby is becoming fiercely independent, wrapped up in their own private world of exploration and adventure – until they need something, be it food or hugs. I am beginning to realise that being a mother is a wait-ing, watching role: I really am at the Emperor's command.

But equally, I know the day I stop worrying I am not doing enough is the day I have become too complacent.

So remember, more often than not, toddler knows best.

Except, of course, when it comes to windows, plugs, wall sock-ets, climbable furniture, eating their bodyweight in chocolate … the list goes on.

24TH FEBRUARY

I have a raging headache. I have too much to do, and I got up late. Two hours of screaming toddler later, I feel as guilty as anything, because I have just asked him to play in his room. As I keep telling you, sometimes it isn't the toddler that needs a time-out, it's you. And as long as his play space is safe, full of toys, you can hear him and he knows you're nearby, it really is OK. Honestly – and that last comment is for me.

4TH MARCH

The Emperor has consistently been asking to have his nappy changed and announcing his poos. So today he sat in the potty seat on the toilet. He enjoyed the experience greatly, but nothing happened, except for me realising that when it does happen the shield guard is next to useless and if I sat opposite him (for encouragement) I would doubtless get it full in the face.

I read online that when training a little boy to urinate standing up, a Cheerio in the bowl gives him an excellent target to aim at. Huh? The Emperor would reach in and eat it.

6TH MARCH

Another intended long stroll has been cut short by the Emperor attempting to hijack passing children's toys. A lot of them, obviously well brought up, offer to share, which is very nice except the Emperor, I know, will never willingly give anything back.

When the Emperor goes off with someone's toy I am obviously embarrassed, but a part of me is proud my child is being so sociable (even if it is in a taxation sort of way). However, when the Emperor offers another child Stinky Bear my heart is in my mouth as to whether this beloved piece of toxic, stuffed material will be returned. (I know the hell our lives will be if Stinky Bear is lost.)

But children (and sometimes their parents too) need to learn to share. If he went to nursery it would be easy, and I'm sure when he does he will learn some hard lessons.

> **THE CONCEPTS OF OWNERSHIP AND SHARING**
>
> Children below the age of three don't really understand the concept of sharing and ownership. 'Mine!' isn't a lot different to 'I want'. They may not be reassured by the promise of a future turn. And they definitely aren't going to understand that the other child wants that toy too.
>
> However by the time they are four they should be able to understand these principles. You can help them now by modelling good behaviour and encouraging them to share toys they are not using. It is wise to limit situations where sharing can cause a problem at this age. (I shouldn't be encouraging him to hand Stinky Bear over to another child. It could all go horribly wrong, and reinforce entirely the wrong ideas.)

On my way home today, one little boy (about seven), whose bicycle the Emperor had tried to steal, stopped me and said in tones of awe, "He really liked my bike, didn't he?"

"Yes," I said, a struggling, drooling, scrabbling Emperor in my arms, "He did. He thinks your bike is very cool."

And the little boy rode off with the biggest grin on his face.

The Emperor had to be placated with crisps.

8ᵀᴴ MARCH

I'm increasingly aware that the Emperor pays more and more attention to what is on TV. As he is entering another I don't like sleeping period, he is awake more evenings. I decided he couldn't see shows that involved overt violence, and especially guns. I now have to tape almost everything I would have previously watched. What shocks me is that I simply didn't realise how prevalent violence is in the shows I favour.

I also decided (being very fond of the tai chi sword form) that swords, staffs, light sabres and the like would be allowed. My thinking was these at least allowed him to learn about the consequences of actions. You can whack someone with a plastic sword and they can whack you back.

I was a little surprised yesterday, when visiting family, to witness the Emperor pluck a stake from the garden and patrol the outside perimeter of the house several times rather proficiently wielding his makeshift staff. Monsters aren't going to cause this little boy nightmares.

10TH MARCH

As I write the Emperor is marauding through his HappyLand Empire. The hospital is getting particularly short shrift; bandaged men and women and emergency services are flying through the air as the ambulance, upside down, nee-nors softly from down the back of the sofa. The x-ray machine is between his teeth. He is like some baby t-rex, trembling with rage and this, I know, is him trying to control his temper. The frantic biting of the nearest toy, complete with head trembling and bulging veins is his way of controlling his frustration – anger management for toddlers. The cause of all this distress? The dog kept falling out of the back of the ambulance (bad dog!) and he isn't strong enough to push down the front of the vehicle to make it sound its siren. He has to rely on me to do this – and sometimes the reliance on Mama is just too much for a young toddler's pride to bear.

11ᵀᴴ MARCH

Hugely significant step forward. I find an affordable play-group he can attend from 30 months. It's very near, very reasonably priced, and will mean we have to get up at the crack of dawn to attend, but it's well worth it. They also ask the mothers to do one session every three weeks.

And so, of course, it's fully booked.

We're on the waiting list for three mornings a week (9am-11.30am), but with all the nursery nurses on strike it could be some time before we get in. (Typically they have a big gap at the end of the summer when many children move into nursery.) I did sound out the play worker on other activities for 28 month olds in the area and, as I suspected, unless I pay to put him into nursery crèche, there isn't anything.

Must put him on a list for nursery at three.

Very confused. He so desperately wants to play with other children (gathering minions for his empire early). I so desperately want some headspace to myself. And yet, I don't want to let him go. These months, no matter how trying they are (and at times they are trying in the same way as the planet Jupiter is a little on the large side to fit in your pocket) are the last few weeks when he and I will be fully immersed in each other's world.

Don't listen to me. By the time he's three, we'll both be gagging to get him into nursery.

NURSERIES, PLAYGROUPS, CHILDMINDERS AND HOME

There are multiple childcare options available. Each offers different benefits and drawbacks, and each suits different families. Cost is always a factor.

Nurseries will take children from four months (and a few from even younger). Children in the UK currently qualify for 12.5 hours a week nursery care from the term after their third birthday. This care has to be in a government partner nursery, a nursery class attached to a primary school, or playgroup. These partners have to conform not only to various safety standards, but they must also follow a recognised curriculum.

Playgroups are typically morning only affairs, run by the local community in conjunction with play workers. Parents can expect to be asked to take part in playgroups, so it does not suit full time working parents. However, these often function as a good introduction to socialising for children who have either a stay at home carer, or one who works part time.

Some playgroups may have an excellent reputation locally but follow no curriculum, so won't qualify to be a partner with the government. There will also be nurseries that are entirely private, which doesn't mean they don't teach the children. In fact they may offer more, but they are not obliged to do so.

You can combine funded government places with self-financing nursery places and/or playgroups. Nursery classes attached to primary schools normally offer care only during school term times.

Child minders are a much more flexible option. Some will come to your home, but most will care for a group of children in their own home. They must be registered (In England with OSFTED, in

Scotland with the Care Commission, in Northern Ireland with the local health and social services trust and in Wales by the Cares Standards Inspectorate).

Alternatively, you can stay at home with your children. This works best if you have friends or family who also have young children who can give you the occasional break, and allow the child to socialise with its peers.

www.childcarelink.gov.uk gives helpful advice and information for England, Wales and Scotland.

15TH MARCH

Let's think about the message I am sending my growingly aware son.

Mama is always here. She will always drop whatever she is doing to play with you. She will feed you, clothe you, bathe you, and any night she goes out comes back guilty and consolatory. She is your constant attendant.

Dada goes to work.

Yes, a lot of the time you see Mama playing with her laptop she is working, but you're not going to understand that for a while, especially as you have a laptop too (although I've yet to see you writing any opuses on your supermarket letter learner).

Sometimes Mama does housework (as infrequently as she can get away with it), but she always picks up your toys, arranges your bed, does your washing and is generally of the inactive (as opposed to going for a run every morning) kind of a woman.

Dada comes home, takes over all the chores and plays riotous games with you, but we all know he's been away doing something important all day. Then often Mama makes tea.

Aargh! I'm setting an example for my son as the woman I always said I would never be.

However much women like me might wish it was otherwise, unless you're prepared (and can afford) to put your child into nursery (and obviously some women have to do this) then the one who stays at home is most likely to be the woman. Not least in all these considerations is that (in the UK at least) men are paid much better than women. A lot is made of mother-baby bonding and, while this is a real phenomenon, I also see no reason why the father-baby bond cannot equally be strengthened by spending time together.

Nursery wasn't an option for me when the Emperor was born. I'd always said I would put my child into nursery, and not doing so was at enormous personal (not financial) cost. I love being with my son, and I will miss him. I know I will regard these times as the most halcyon of days in hindsight, and not the three years of cribbed, sanity sucking confinement it has been. I love being with him, but in that age old dilemma I also love being me.

GENDER MODELLING – OR NATURE VERSUS NURTURE

In gender as in everything else nature has a plan for your toddler, but she isn't telling. Likewise it is also true that as parents we can encourage specific behaviours and patterns of association. Little boys may be naturally boyish, and little girls may gravitate towards dolls, but we can encourage our children to keep an open mind towards gender roles in society, for example, not all nurses are female, not all mothers are the main childcarer. It is important not to reinforce society led stereotypes.

On the other hand, it also isn't worth deliberately trying to turn your life upside down by, say, insisting all household chores are rotated between parents to accomplish this. If you have a happy, well functioning household where everyone feels their role is valued and supported then you're doing a great job of modelling how individuals can get along together, which is no small life lesson.

However, if one parent is left to do all the housework, all the dull chores and (naturally) resents this, then you are modelling an astonishingly bad set of roles. Children need to perceive give and take between the sexes. Be wary of ever explaining Mama/Dada does this because s/he is a woman/man, or by your actions allowing your toddler to leap to this conclusion.

21ST MARCH Mothers' Day

Books, cards, candlelit baths and Love Actually on DVD, and nothing to do. This is what motherhood is all about.

23RD MARCH

I'm rubbing arnica cream on my bruises and thinking about self-protection and toddlers. This will only make sense as time moves on, but as my friend Tracy says, "They have baby websites where they email you weekly updates the stages your baby is at. There should be one that emails you with warnings: baby now able to headbutt, baby will now bite everything it can get in its mouth, take your earrings out or risk a ripped ear, keep shins away from babies feet, beware flying objects like saucepans..."

Injuries caused by toddlers to people I know include broken noses, dislocated jaws, countless bruises, sprains and muscle strains as well as a broken collar bone and broken fingers. As another of my friends (whose toddler broke her nose twice) Clare puts it, "Toddlers, as well as their toys, need warning labels."

27ᵀᴴ MARCH

Today was a special day; the Emperor ate a reasonably sized piece of boiled potato. His face while chewing and swallowing did suggest I had fed him the contents of the cats' litter tray, but he didn't spit it out.

28ᵀᴴ MARCH

Today we finally made it to the local soft play centre – a gym hall filled with lots of foam filled shapes and a bouncy castle. For the first half of his hour slot there was no one there apart from his father and me. (I own a certain amount of guilt that I didn't buy Dada a child's ticket too. Although he was too big to get on the bouncy castle, he had a lot of fun; even demonstrating cartwheels to a bemused toddler, who quite reasonably felt running around on his feet up and down foam stairs was more than enough, and if he had to learn about walking on his hands too he really should have been given more notice.)

Thirty minutes later another child a few months younger is brought in by his parents. The Emperor, despite being hampered by a lack of nursery contact, is immediately up and away, babbling to the other child. The two of them point, chuckle, take turns at chasing each other, and generally co-operate in playing in a manner that appears to give the lie to a lot of established child psychology which suggests very young children are incapable of co-operation. The Emperor, it is soon clear, is a leader.

This becomes even more apparent when an older woman arrives (about three and a half at a guess) and he immediately forsakes his new playmate to fetch her plastic play balls, offering them up as respectfully as any Victorian suitor ever offered flowers. Abandoned, the other little boy runs back to his mum for juice and parental encouragement.

SOCIALISATION

It's amazing how children interact with each other. The Emperor has a small friend, about seven months his junior, whose first language is German. The two of them communicate with a series of strange noises, and what his mother and I can only describe as penguin impressions.

Interacting with those of their own age is an entirely different experience for your child from being with you. The experience not only builds social skills, but confidence, communication skills and awareness. There are no superficial barriers when you're two and three. Children will happily interact with each other at playgroups, play parks and soft play centres despite never having previously met. Even at this age, your toddler is capable of finding his own friends, and while some of these relationships may last no longer than a couple hours others may build into regular contacts for both of you. Either way, both experiences are an essential part of growing up.

1ST APRIL

Err, this isn't a joke. It looks like the Emperor may not remain an only child after all. Oh, wow, does he have a shock coming.

4TH APRIL

The Emperor has started taking afternoon naps once more. This is so relaxing. At the moment I'm finding three to four hours of intensive toddler time is as much as I can take without a small break.

7TH APRIL

I appear still to be pregnant, which is continuing to surprise me. Having been assured by several doctors I would never have children the Emperor was a delightful surprise, but to do it again, although still delightful, is decidedly brain numbing.

I'm also becoming more and more aware of the stages I want to get the Emperor through before baby no. 2 arrives. Top of my list of priorities is potty training or, as I have foolishly hoped to scale this problem in a single bound (like the super-hero the advertising world now seems bent on telling mothers we are), go straight to toilet training.

It's not going well. I bought a toilet seat but, once on the pot, it slithers and slides like an eel in butter. Not that it matters: apart from being somewhat bemused and interested to be placed on a porcelain throne, the Emperor is not performing.

I think modern nappies are just too comfortable. I ask you, what is the incentive to learn to use the toilet when you have a convenient disposal system that means you don't have to interrupt your play?

8ᵀᴴ APRIL

"Are you being a parrot today?"

"Pawot?"

"Repeating everything I say?"

"Wpeawing."

"Isn't this a little dull?"

"Dull?"

"So is this you trying to learn words?"

"Learn words."

"OK, let's try some." (Me pointing at nearby things.)

"OK."

"Ball."

"Ball."

"Bear."

"Bear."

"Dinosaur."

"Dinosaw."

"Laptop."

"Laptop, puter."

"Window."

"Indow."

"Tricycle."

"Aaaaaaaaaarh! Cat!"

(Cat streaks along the hallway followed by the Emperor's maniacal laughter.)

"Yes, that was the cat. Poor cat."

"Poor cat" (more laughter).

"OK, time for me to go get your lunch."

"Get lunch."

"What would you like?"

"What would you like?"

"Something nice and healthy?"

"NAH! Biscuit."

I swear he understands every word I say.

11ᵀᴴ APRIL

Easter Sunday

"Is he pointing Percy at the porcelain yet?" asks my father.

When will he ever be potty trained?

14ᵀᴴ APRIL

I had thought for a few weeks that the Emperor was not going to be an only child. However, the pregnancy is now failing.

When I thought I was going to have a child in November, I was panicking over whether I would have the Emperor toilet trained by then. I was concerned how I would deal with his more frequent little tantrums without resorting to picking him up. Now, the overwhelming feeling is sadness, and although I have tried not to show my tears in front of my son, he has been remarkably well behaved: going quietly to bed, eating his meals for once (he even bit into an apple, although he quickly spat it out again), but more than anything I have been overwhelmed by offers of 'Big hugs'.

I didn't know two year olds could be so sensitive.

27ᵀᴴ APRIL

I am waiting for the terrorist prevention squad to arrive. I cannot believe the toxic fumes coming out of the Emperor's nappies; nor how he can be so oblivious to it. I have produced a child who has no sense of smell.

I need to think about toilet training – or not so much think as do. I don't feel quite ready to cope with what seems like climbing a mountain at present. A small molehill would defeat me today. I've had the all clear on the miscarriage. My body has gone back to normal, but my mind is taking a while to catch up.

Sadly, being trained in this area, I know rationally what it is going on. This doesn't make anything any better. It does allow me to feel infuriated by a call from the local health visitor, who in a very short space of time was so condescending and displayed such a terrible idea of good practice that if I had been her supervisor I would have smacked her round the head. Deep breaths. However, I was extremely pleased to hear that the miscarriage support line, whose number the hospital gave me, also listens to fathers.

3RD MAY

A bank holiday weekend, and living by the seaside I feel the urge to do something holidayish with the Emperor, which resolves itself into daily trips to the play park. This time with two of us fielding he only tries to walk on air three dozen or so times. Children six months younger than him can manage the slide, but not the Emperor. The sheer joy and pleasure of being active, the cries of the other children around him and the sunny day, spur him on to beliefs in his own superpowers. He races up the steps, reaches the top of the slide (which has large, helpful safety rails, which he ignores) and launches himself, sometimes still standing, at the chute. This self-jettisoning is frequently inaccurate and results in him dangling in mid-air suspended by either his father's hand or mine on the back of his jacket. So here's my problem: how is he going to learn any sense of danger if he doesn't understand the consequences and doesn't appreciate not all the world is a soft play centre? He has no fear. Oh no, all that fear has been transplanted into my heart, as I watch my tiny daredevil throw himself into play with the fierce single-mindedness of a triathlete training for the toddler olympics. There were children of 14 months using the slide; cautiously, carefully, thoughtfully, urged on by a loving parent. And then there was the Emperor, all 12kg of him, barrelling up the steps, using his feet, hands and occasionally his face for extra purchase.

When we leave the play park there is much screaming, wailing, lashing of feet and other displays typical of a toddler learning the world is not fair, and that he can't do what he wants every single moment of every single day.

It says a lot that this now seems perfectly normal to me.

6TH MAY

Yesterday morning I woke up and realised that some of my MS symptoms had returned. Considering the stress of the miscarriage it's not surprising, but I opted for an emergency GP appointment after the Emperor said, "Don't cry Mama." I so don't want him to have this image of a miserable stay at home mother, because I'm not. But I know the way memory works he will remember the unusual or emotionally charged parts of his early life more clearly than the smooth normality.

At the GPs he met and played with (actually played with) several other children. They all gathered round the gigantic wire and bead table, which is designed to torment people with migraines. With one little nine month old boy the Emperor crouched down, much as I have to do with him, and asked the child, "Are you OK? Do you understand? Do you want to see how it works?" I was so proud of him – and to think I used to be worried about his language. He then spoilt the impression a little by turning to the baby's mother, pointing at her shoes and yelling, "Disgusting!", which is a new favourite word. But then I guess it's his job to embarrass me and at least he didn't treat the other children the way he insists on treating our cats.

10TH MAY

The Emperor is two and a half today.

REVIEW: HALF WAY THROUGH THE TERRIBLE TWOS

MY GOALS

1 By the time he is three the Emperor will be eating a healthy mixed diet without complaint, and pudding bribes will be a thing of the past.

He did eat that bit of boiled potato, but nothing has really changed. 6/10

2 Nappies will be a dim memory, with all bodily waste products going in the loo, without having to go through the hell of pottydom.

We do have a toilet seat, and he has sat on it. No change. 2/10

3 Every night the Emperor will go down for at least 10 hours of undisturbed rest.

No change – still failing with regular bedtimes. 7/10

4 As mother I will continually strive to provide entertainment and activities suitable for the Emperor's developing mind and body (which includes ethically correct selection of toys and television programmes).

We're doing quite a lot more playing together as he begins to show an interest in games. 6/10

5 I will begin the socialisation process of the Emperor by finding him other children to play with, and cease surrounding him totally with servile adults.

We're booked into playgroup. He's mixing with other children at play sessions and at the play park. 6/10

6 At the end of the year, the Emperor will be able to give his real name and address when asked, and will be fluent in conversational adult-speak.

The address isn't going so well, but he is beginning to be able to chat. 6/10

7 I will ensure that the Emperor's surroundings are safe, and that we never have another occurrence of the collapsed babygate and the stairs.

Fingers crossed no change. 10/10

8 I will undertake to school the Emperor in the ways of acceptable behaviour without resorting to corporal punishment, or anything that may entail long term therapy (for either of us) at a later date.

I don't think things have got any worse, but they haven't got any better. 5/10

9 I will not work full time. I will devote huge amounts of each day to the caring of the Emperor and his environs, but I will

also write, study and achieve a minimal level of social life.

No change. I'm sure in a previous life I had friends. 6/10

10 I will not be a sucker for the Emperor's huge blue topaz eyes or other formidable weapons in his armoury of manipulation and cajolement.

As if. 4/10

THE EMPEROR'S GOAL

1 To bend the known universe to his will.

He's still winning. 6/10

AND THE DETAILED HALF YEARLY REPORT

Hygiene

TOILET TRAINING

Despite an early creative and innovative flair in the 'wee' department, the Emperor shows no real interest in this area. (When around 18 months the Emperor managed to pull down his nappy and trousers in order to wee on his own head by dint of careful aiming and by way of a posture which is normally the province of yogis.)

Toilet training has to wait until the child is ready. It's perfectly OK to be toilet training at 3.

TEETH CLEANING

'Brushy teeth' is one of the Emperor's favourite activities. He has one toothbrush. I have the other. The biggest problem now is he wants to clean his teeth entirely on his own.

By this time a child should be brushing their teeth twice a day, using a pea sized amount of child's toothpaste. You should brush their teeth for them as well as them doing it for themselves, as they may not be too thorough. Your child's first trip to the dentist should be when they are around two to three, unless there are problems. Check with your own dentist when they like to start.

HAND WASHING

'Washy hands' is another favourite pastime.

This means you can use it as a 'bribe' to encourage your child to use the potty or toilet and wash their hands afterwards. Ideally this should be a routine after using the potty, before eating food and whenever finishing more messy play or returning from an outdoor trip where leaves, pebbles and other such things have been acquired.

NAIL CLIPPING

Rather like the puppy he often pretends to be, the Emperor tends to wear his nails down. This is not ideal, but prevents me potentially mutilating him when I try to clip these. It does mean that I have to ensure his nails are clean.

HAIR WASHING

We have passed the screaming and throwing things around whenever water gets near his eyes. Baths are now a learning experience: what floats, how much water will go in what, and how wet can I get my washer?

Bath time is also often Dada time. Leaving aside that Dada does a much better game of pirates than me, this is one of the necessary but fun times that gives the office bound Dada some serious playtime with his son.

BATHS

How often can you wash a toddler before he shrinks? As often as is necessary to dislodge grime, and as they get older this will become more frequent. However, toddlers have sensitive skins that over-bathing or harsh cleaning agents can dry out. Here, at least the Emperor is progressing well. He loves baths. The drawback is he has so much energy that a daily bath and his parents' sanity are rarely compatible.

Despite what they said in the fifties a bit of dirt doesn't kill a toddler. If both you and your child are exhausted by the end of the day it's probably better for both of you not to go for the bath option. Just like babies, toddlers have to be watched every minute. Toddlers are active and adventurous, testing the boundaries of their environment. (How much do you hate being told that every five minutes by everyone?) A bath is a brilliant place to learn about letters by using those foam ones that stick with water onto tiles. (I'm less sure about bath crayons, as I suspect these would encourage the Emperor to crayon on living room and bedroom walls.) Bath time is an ideal opportunity for learning about empty and full – cleaned and delabelled plastic bottles are perfect for this. Toddlers can explore the beginnings of science by learning what floats. Also from very early on they can have a perceived level of autonomy, by washing themselves with a washmit or bodyscrunch.

HAIRCUTS (OR NOT)

The key in this area was finding a stylist who not only understood the Emperor's image, but also allowed him to pretend her hair clips were warring dinosaurs.

Clippers are a lot safer than scissors. Some children like the feel on their head; others detest it. Many hairdressers will see children from 24 months and up. Check before you bring your child in. Usual procedure will be to have your toddler sit on your lap, while the hairdresser chops. Be aware that fees for children's haircuts are typically static, so if you toddler has one centimetre that needs trimming, it will cost as much as the 10 year old girl who requires a complicated style.

Feeding

FOOD AND FUSSY EATING

No change. My son exists on cheerios, toast, crisps, rusks, chocolate, full fat milk and fruit juice. He is offered many other things, but all other foods are suspect. Occasionally he will now dip his crisps or breadsticks. He likes salsa.

DIETARY WORRIES

Although he isn't eating what I would like, the Emperor is actually getting the dietary requirements he needs.

MOVING TOWARDS CUPS (OR DON'T EAT THAT STRAW)

This morning the Emperor was found filling his hollow toy knights from his juice bottle to drink out of them. He is getting the idea of cups, but as this is cranberry season, it's a very messy learning curve.

Ideally fruit juice should always been given in a cup rather than a bottle. If your child has frequent citric or added sugar drinks during the day, encouraging them to use a straw helps protect their teeth.

CUTLERY SKILLS

He can use my cutlery just fine.

Around now children can manage spoons and forks – cutting with a knife is harder. One of those dual purpose fork and spoons also helps the transition to using a fork.

Social skills

MEETING OTHER CHILDREN AND INTERACTING NICELY

The few times the Emperor has been in contact with other children, he has been very well behaved, even bringing the little girls gifts. However, he is not a follower, he takes charge of games and very much does his own thing. I wonder what will happen when he is around very much bigger children.

SEPARATION ANXIETY

So far the Emperor has been left only with people he knows well. As such he has shown no separation anxiety. A few days ago a favourite adult was away for a while, and he showed concern this person had been locked in the garden shed. However when they reappeared he accepted their arrival quite happily. He likes people to say goodbye to him and let them know if they will be back 'soon', 'later' or, favourite of all, 'very soon'.

If a special person is going away for a time, and the child is already concerned about the impending absence, then it can help to exchange items such as a photo or a cuddly toy for each other to look after. This is a promise and reassurance of return. However, this is a second line of attack. If your child isn't overly worried (or as worried as the person leaving) by the forthcoming trip don't use this technique. It will only focus attention on the departure.

LANGUAGE

The Emperor can now repeat anything (which means I really have to watch my language around him).

INTERACTION WITH SIGNIFICANT ADULTS

The Emperor is definitely worse with me than with his Dada. He also sees his mother at home for most of the day, while his father goes off to work. Mother may be working harder than she can describe in toddler appropriate language, but that isn't how he sees it. I am here for his convenience.

Role modelling is beginning to become a serious issue (at least in my mind).

PETS AND THE ROAMING TODDLER

The cats are packed – they just can't reach the latch. I'll be surprised if they both stay through the summer.

TODDLER TANTRUMS

* Violence towards parents
  Check

- Throwing heavy things
  Check

- Refusing to move
  Check

- Prolonged crying
  Check

- Sulking
  Check

- Hitting/biting other children
  So far bitten only his father and grandfather.

A pretty full check on all normal toddler tantrums.

HOW MUCH ATTENTION IS ENOUGH?

I'm beginning to wonder too.

Self-discovery

The Emperor is showing a desire to crawl under women's skirts and to also grab a handful of breast given the slightest opportunity. Mostly, he is doing this with me. He doesn't often take his clothes off. (My American friend with twins came through one morning to find both children with their nappies off, and that the girl had smeared her whole crib liberally with poo.) He also likes to play with tugboat Willy in the bath – and you've guessed right, there is no boat there.

As I said at the start lots of people will tell you what to do, but in the end it's down to you. This is my take on a very difficult situation.

The key with dealing with this interest in the human form is (as usual) with toddlers not to show too much interest. There is nothing so much fun to your tiny tyrant as a display of horror and shock. Explain that it is polite to keep your clothes on in front of other people and that no clothes is reserved for the bath. Answer any questions your child has about the way their body works (where does the poo come out, for example). Explain that other people don't like to be poked, prodded or investigated any more than the toddler would, and it is not nice to hoist up women's skirts to see what colour underwear they have. Always answer questions honestly but with minimal detail; don't give your child any more information than they need at any one time.

It's a fine line between preventing your toddler from becoming a social outcast and dampening their natural curiosity.

It's also the time to start thinking about nudity around your toddler. Sadly, this is the kind of thing we do have to worry about today. You will need to decide on your own guideline. If you continue having baths together the important thing is for your child to understand that while it is OK to share a bath with Mama or Dada, and allow them or other known babysitters to dress and undress them, it is not OK for anyone else to do this. The easiest way to put it is along the lines of "You know how you're not allowed to look up Auntie Maureen's dress? Well, no one is allowed to look up yours either. It's all about being nice to people". (Obviously you have to fit the gender to the example.)

It's really hard to do and appals me that I have to mention this kind of thing at all. Frankly, I do not believe there is a child molester around every corner but, I am horrified to say, I do think we have to prepare our children about what is acceptable behaviour from other adults. I also don't think parents, especially fathers, should worry about bathing their own girl toddlers; that's taking things way too far.

I do not believe it does any good to frighten children or tell them tales of monsters. The best way to protect your child is to ensure you only leave them with people you know well and you check out all nursery schools very thoroughly.

Responsible adult supervision is the best way to keep your toddler safe.

Play

I'm learning that there are days when however much I play with the Emperor it is never enough. Also he can be quite happy playing on his own until I start working, then suddenly he wants to climb into my lap or onto my laptop.

I will always feel I never give him enough time, and then there will be days when he wants nothing to do with me.

A toddler needs help playing, and he needs to make discoveries on his own.

READING

We spend a lot of time reading. Reading him stories above anything else has helped him develop language skills. As well as the inevitable Maisy Mouse books, his father has been reading him The Hobbit at bedtime.

Children like bright, incredibly repetitive books to read along with, especially ones about doing very ordinary things they can relate to. They also like to hear your voice, and hearing complex language is not a bad thing. They don't need to understand it all, but a lot of it does get stored up. A book like The Hobbit may not be appropriate reading for all toddlers, but if your child enjoys it then go ahead, so long as it's not at the expense of picture books.

If your child is watching you read, run your finger under the words as you read them – it teaches them that we read from left to right.

REPETITIVE PLAY

Repetitive play with sand, water, bottles, or simply putting things inside other things and taking them out, is about learning. Earnestly balancing blocks is the equivalent of an afternoon at the stock market for a toddler. They are learning all the time.

ACTIVITIES

Here the Emperor doesn't score too highly. He's great at playing in the back garden, riding in his buggy and socialising with my adult friends. However, taking him for walks, down to the beach or to the shops on my own is a nightmare. He is happy until his wishes and mine no longer coincide. Then he screams, drops to the floor and refuses to move. I'm working on this by making sure we have outings with his Dada, but on his own my very strong and strong willed little boy is not easy to manage outside the home. For those of you with more amiable toddlers I recommend the local library, town hall, Internet and sports centres for information on outside activities. If you have a wilful child like mine you can hope, as I do, that nursery will help socialise them.

LEARNING TO SWIM

We haven't even started, but we should have. Most public baths will have parent and child lessons for very young children.

Safety

THE STUFF OF NIGHTMARES

Despite the best laid plans, children do hurt themselves. If I listed everything they could harm themselves with it would take this entire book.

The obvious indoor things are cables, electricity, fire, water, drops/gaps, medicines, hot things (tea, pans, ovens, kettles etc), bins, household cleaners, open windows/doors, glass panels (cover with special clear plastic to prevent shattering), and small objects that can be swallowed.

Outside almost everything seems a threat, from strangers to cars. Toddlers need to be restrained near traffic, bridges and in crowded areas, in a buggy, held by their hand or with a wrist strap or reins, unless you are in a park where it is safe for them to play. (And then you have to watch they don't throw themselves off a slide or fall into ponds.)

Nothing beats keeping an eye on them, and when you can't they need to be in as safe an environment as you can manage.

Your mission, which you must accept, is to keep them safe without making them afraid. Forethought in the removal of dangers is the best way possible.

INSIDE THE CAR

Toddlers must have specially fitted seats. They must never, under any circumstance, be sat on someone's lap or sat in an adult seat. Travelling in either of these ways means in any accident it is likely they would die.

Sleep

BEDTIME ROUTINES

We do have a near ritual reading of *How Do Dinosaurs Say Good Night?* which means the day is finally over, but I'm not being good at all at regular bedtimes.

By now a toddler should have a regular bedtime routine.

NIGHTMARES AND NIGHT TERRORS

I've been very lucky the Emperor has only had a couple of nightmares. Some children are unlucky enough to have night terrors.

It's always disturbing for parents when their children have bad dreams, and there is a tendency to wonder what happened to make their dreams so nasty. Children on the edge of language dream about all sorts of things they cannot explain. There are a thousand and one things going through their young minds: a lost toy, a grazed knee, a misunderstanding; all these are the stuff of bad dreams.

Here are some solutions to try – you shouldn't need to use them all. Pick the ones that will help you and your child.

- *Nightmares can be particularly challenging for toddlers who may not be able to distinguish the dream from reality.*

- *Talking about fears in the daytime helps, and also avoiding frightening or violent media.*

- *Reassure your child that dreams cannot harm them. It may help to explain about dreams being inside their head. Some children may also respond to the idea that they can tell bad dreams to go away. Other, less confident children may respond to being told they can tell a bad dream firmly: "Mummy/Daddy says you must go away" and it will go away. In this case you would aim to move to the child taking the initiative in telling it to go away over time. To avoid a child believing they can wish away a real dangerous situation (such as fire) these approaches are best suited to toddlers who can tell the difference between dreams and real life. However, if your child's nightmares are always about dinosaurs or something they are equally unlikely to encounter in reality, you can make the instruction explicitly specific to the cause: "When the (insert impossible threat of your child's choice) comes back tell it Mummy/Daddy/you says it must go away, and it will."*

- *If your child is frightened of monsters or something similarly frightening under the bed or in the wardrobe, you can open the window and chase it out and then close the window. Be very assertive and tell the monster "We don't allow monsters in this house. Go out and don't ever come back in." Give your child confidence that you are in charge and monsters hold no fear so long as you are there. You can progress this to allowing the child to chase out the monster – a very empowering technique (and one at which the Emperor excels).*

- *Don't spend ages searching the room for imaginary creatures, though. The important thing is to convince your child that it wouldn't matter if there were a monster there – you're in charge and that means your child is safe.*

- *Some parents use such things as dreamcatchers. This can work for children whose fears will disappear if they only believe they will. However be wary of going down this path or you may end up with dreamcatchers, worry dolls, and a teenager who always wants something or somebody to make things better. (It's fine for Mum and Dad to be heroes when you are very young, but as they grow children have to internalise that sense of safety and protection.)*

- *If a nightmare continues and is affecting the child's daytime behaviour then it is time to see a doctor.*

While a nightmare is a regular dream with frightening content, a night terror is a sleep pathology (related to sleep walking). A parent will be summoned into the room by anguished cries and/or terrified screams to find their child sometimes standing, with eyes wide open, but unable to recognise them and still asleep. In these cases the event is often most frightening for the parent and is normally not even remembered by the child. Strangely this is an inherited phenomenon and appears unrelated to daytime stresses.

A child having a night terror is trapped in a limbo world between waking and sleeping which is very frightening for them. The aim is either

to allow them to wake up (from where they can get back to sleep peace-
fully) or ease them back into relaxed sleep mode. If you find your child
in the midst of a night terror:

- *You may be unable to wake them. If you want to try, either turn on*
  the lights or apply a cold wet flannel to their wrists or forehead.

- *If they get out of bed, gently guide them back (to avoid injury).*

- *If your child is not wearing nappies they may well need to pee so*
  encourage them to do this.

- *Talk in a calm soothing way.*

- *If your child wakes with night terrors at a regular time, you may be*
  able to break the pattern. Sit by their bedside shortly before their nor-
  mal night terror time. As it begins, their breathing rate and pulse
  rate will increase. When you notice this happening, wake them
  before the terror starts.

- *Sleep deprivation is a common cause of night terrors. If your tod-*
  dler is prone to these try to avoid letting them become over tired.

- *If a night terror is accompanied by jerking, drooling or other signs*
  of seizure consult a doctor.

DISTURBED SLEEP (FOR EVERYONE)

Now this is something the Emperor and I are doing well with.
If he wakes and is disturbed, or refuses to settle, then I will
return to check on him and give him a big hug, but I will not
stay no matter how much his blue topaz eyes fill with tears or
his angelic bottom lip trembles. This is one area where he
hasn't got me on a string.

As ever – do not reward inappropriate behaviour.

THE MOTHER'S REVIEW

BEING YOURSELF

It is so easy to lose your identity with a small child. Even going to the shops becomes a major outing, as opposed to popping round the corner. Regardless of whether you're a full time mum or working it is important to find time to be yourself. The hardest part of this is it often means you must socialise without your best friend, the father of your toddler. Parents' romantic lives are curtailed in so many different ways. Early bedtime routines give you a little time to yourselves, and if you have willing grandparents, then maybe you will manage the odd weekend away together.

No matter how much you all love each other, young children are often cited as the cause of break-ups. Don't let this be you. You need to give each other space, and also allow each of you out on your own to pursue hobbies and interests. It's a big juggling act. You need time with your partner and no child, time with your child and no partner, time alone, and time together as a family.

WHAT IS A GOOD ENOUGH MOTHER?

One who stays reasonably sane despite her tiny tyrant and whose toddler is, in between the tantrums, happy.

17TH MAY

So now he's two and a half he should be going to playgroup, and he should be registered for nursery, if not primary school too. I am a bad mother ™.

CHOOSING A NURSERY

Visit your nursery by all means. Check their space and creden-
tials. But if you're cynical like me and think having mostly pre-ver-
bal clients could put you on to a nice little earner, then word of
mouth is the most reliable source. If a mother can tell me her
child has been there for a reasonably long period of time and is
yet to sustain a serious injury or life threatening illness and is
socialising well, then I am more likely to consider this as an option.
Where I live we are surrounded by nurseries, some of them in the
most marvellous buildings. However, having spoken to local people the one most likely to enjoy the Emperor's patronage is the
least prepossessing of all the local buildings.

I don't believe the Emperor will have separation anxiety, but
his mother will. Yesterday, he had his first ever ice cream cone
at the beach, and shortly after he'd begun I had to leave to
make a meeting. So I left the cutest little thing ever munching
and enjoying his first treat-and-beach experience; I was gutted.
The Emperor on the other hand, who was sitting on a wall
with his father watching the lady-babies, said "Bye-bye Mama"
and tucked into his cone without a second glance. I tried to be
pleased about this (and failed).

SEPARATION ANXIETY

A phenomenon investigated by, among others, a psychologist
called Bowlby; this is basically about children missing their primary carers. Obviously, if your child is delighted to see you
depart, then things are very wrong. However, showing pleasure
at a new situation and acting in a manner which assumes your
safe return later is the best outcome.

Children have to get used to separation all the time. Every time they go down to sleep, even though you remain in the house, they are being left. It's all about trust, and you can work on separation anxiety long before they go to nursery.

Never just disappear. Always say goodbye

As children get older it becomes more important that they know the person in whose care they are being left. You can leave a very small child with a caring babysitter, but toddlers want to know what is going on. Where is Mama going? Where is Dada? Explain, even if you don't think they'll understand all the words. Explain you are going and you will be back soon – or later. (Differentiate between short and longer absences.) Give a kiss and a hug – do not pander to tears. Once you have said you are going, go or the child will cry more in the hope of getting you to stay. As your child comes to understand that you do come back and that there are fun things they can do without you, then separation anxiety lessens.

In the case of nursery do, if at all possible, take your child to the nursery for a visit, and stay with them. Later you can discuss what an exciting place it is, with so many fun things to do.

Above all when you do take your child to nursery do not show distress, worry or fear at leaving them

Wait until you are outside the gates before you break down and weep like a small child. Separation anxiety is not reserved for small children, and if you have been a mostly stay at home parent the shock is liable to be severe. If possible arrange for coffee with a friend or some other treat the first day you leave them. And of course make sure your mobile is fully charged.

20TH MAY

The Emperor – oh, how I regret that foolish nickname – is spitting, biting, pinching, kicking and generally disregarding me. Of course he doesn't do this all the time, but I feel as if I have lost control. When his father returns home, he is as good as gold for most of the evening. He can't quite make it through the whole evening, and has no chance of being good for an entire weekend, so his true colours are revealed to others.

I think partly this is due to boredom. He is fed up being with Mama. He wants more – and quite rightly so. He is always delighted to see me in the morning and usually affectionate during the day and at bedtime. I admit these times often have a direct correlation to chocolate and stories, but I do believe he loves me.

He has a temper, and somehow I have to find a way to help him work things out. And he is cunning. Recently after a very trying day his father came home and, while helping clear up, told him to sit in a chair and stay there. When his father left the room he ignored my protests, and ran about. When his father came back he leapt into the chair, proudly announced, "Stayed there!" and gave the sweetest smile.

29TH MAY

So I've been to visit a nursery. It does have government funded places and the staff all seem very nice. That's the straightforward bit, the rest is complicated. Not least of which is I thought I had asked all the right questions until I read the council handbook they had given me to take away. Several parents had suggested this particular nursery, which is really the best recommendation. It was definitely staffed by Grannies Inc (the average age of staff being at least 50). The corridors were tiny and the rooms, though adequate, very small. The toys and props were safe, but cheap and cheerful. Everywhere there was children's artwork, and the children were all peaceful and content. The Emperor crossed the room, picked out the best toys, and then joined a drawing table, proceeding to show a child at least a year older how to draw more neatly. When we went next door to look at the Messy Room (which I know he's going to love), he didn't make a noise.

I remember thinking how secure the front door (a double porch) was, but now I'm thinking about the smallness of the corridors and how would they all get out in a fire.

And the price, ye gods above, it's staggering. A full time place would cost as much as a medium mortgage.

THINGS TO ASK YOUR NURSERY

Learning

What are the planned activities? Is there a weekly or monthly curriculum you can see? Is the material on display created by adults or children?

Physical

Are there opportunities to run around and become extremely tired, so the toddlers will go to bed nice and early when you come home, allowing you that glass of wine? Or, more correctly, children develop a lot of their co-ordination around this time, balancing, catching balls, games and so on will not only help keep them fit, but help them develop the skills they need to move their bodies efficiently.

Culture

Or do they only celebrate Christmas? If you want your child to be part of our multicultural society, then you do have to ask. It's a tricky question and difficult to phrase without seeming as if you are asking to see the token ethnic child. This is why I ask about festivals. All institutions have an underlying belief system, which includes atheism.

Qualifications

Who has what?

Staff

Consistency of care. Locally some of the prettiest nurseries have a large through rate of staff. Personally, I'm happier not only if my child gets to know the staff, but also if the nursery manager really knows her staff too. Also, what is the ratio of staff to children?

Food

What is supplied and what do you supply?

Sleeping Space

Some nurseries have nap spaces, others don't.

Security of Premises
Cost

Obvious question, but important.

1ˢᵀ JUNE

Toddlers have their uses. I obtained complete forgiveness for not posting a birthday card by getting the Emperor to leave a Happy Birthday message on an answering machine. Last night he charmed several of my childless friends by his cuteness, hugging and explaining about 'brushy teeth'. Of course none of them are here the next morning when he does his regular poo-of-doom, usually just after we've eaten breakfast.

However, this doesn't inure me to his charms. I'm still prevaricating over this nursery business.

Part of it is simply the pleasure I derive from being with him, despite the kicks, punches to the throat and poos-of-doom. I know he won't love and rely on me in quite the same ways as he gets older. For now I am Mama, who can make the darkest day seem bright, protect him from the ills of the world and always fix a beloved toy. As he grows older I will have to pass my crown to schoolteachers, peers and one day to whomever his heart chooses, but this is my time. I am Mama and there will never be another year like this.

3RD JUNE

Please disregard yesterday's entry. This afternoon:

First there was the explosion of the sand and water table. He was looking so cute if messy as he played that I took a phone photo. While I was figuring how to send it off to his Dada the table and several chairs became covered with very messy sand and water.

"Aw, sorry Mama," says the Angel and as soon as I accept his apology does it all over again.

At this point I decide it's time to go inside.

The Emperor disagrees.

In the end I lure the sand and water swamp monster inside with a choccy-pop. When we get to his bedroom gate he knows if he goes in this will be the end of 'outside', and he looks at me to let me know he knows what I'm planning, but he goes for the choccy-pop anyway. Some things are stronger than freedom.

While he's eating I start changing his clothes, but he is so sodden a bath is going to be the only cure. So I leave him in his nappy and go away to run a bath. I fill it full of bubbles and toys, reckoning it was at least half my fault for taking my eye off him for those moments when the mess assumed mudslide proportions. Downstairs I can hear an angry little boy protesting he wants 'outside'.

I am confronted by a horrid smell. I'm ready to skin the cats alive until I see not only is the nappy on the changing mat, but there are telltale signs of the Emperor's activities. He has peed on the floor twice and followed this up with an encore. From the expression on his face I suspect a prison protest.

After a clean up, a rather cold and distant Mama, who is desperately resisting the urge to lock him in the cupboard under the stairs, takes him off to his bath.

In the bath, he has realised something is up, or rather that he has gone too far this time, and offers me several of his favourite toys saying "It's for you."

I'm not taken in and surprise, surprise we have a tantrum when it's time to come out. A nap is definitely in order to save both our sanities, so off to his bedroom, and just as I am thinking what a cruel mother I am for putting him down for a nap and not continuing to play despite his appalling behaviour, he figures where he is going and tries to bite me.

And the worst of this? He doesn't behave like this for anyone else. It's just for me.

I feel, yet again, as if I am losing control.

8ᵀᴴ JUNE

One mother I know has a three year old daughter who never sleeps. She is separated from the child's father, and so gets to sleep when her daughter goes to visit her father. Other than this she is in a state of permanent sleep deprivation.

SLEEP

Every day ends with a recital of the wonderful *How Do Dinosaurs Say Good Night?,* but the time of the recital varies. A regular bedtime is important. What I should do is put him down at the same time every night, read his story, and then do that sensible thing where if he cries I go and give him a hug to tell him I'm around, and then leave him be.

I used to be good at this. The big eyes, the 'Big Hug Mama', the trembling lip and the quiveringly offered Stinky Bear (I love you so much I'd let you hold my only companion and comrade against the darkness) are winning me over far too often.

So nowadays I don't even try to put him down until he starts to flag. I can't stress how much this is the wrong thing to do.

I do this to avoid distress. It's a common failure among parents who spend all day with their child and really cannot stand any more evening tears. I'm shattered by the end of the day, even if he isn't.

- If your child has a nap during the day keep it before 2 or 3pm.

- Set a regular bedtime routine, at a time that suits everyone, and stick to it.

- Try to ensure your bedtime ritual ends before your child falls asleep. Awakening alone after being read or rocked to sleep can cause distress.

- Follow the bedtime ritual and don't respond to a fuss, as this will encourage more fussing. For example, if your toddler refuses to lie down, explain it is bedtime and calmly leave the room.

- You do need to use your judgement to tell if a child is fussing or is genuinely distressed.

Here's what some experts recommend if your child makes a fuss about being left at bedtime:

- If your child cries, leave for five minutes. Then return, briefly reassure them and leave again.

- This time leave them for 10 minutes. If they are still crying, again return to reassure them briefly, then leave.

- Increase the time you are away by five minutes each time.

- It's important that you remain calm (easier said than done), have minimal physical contact and give brief reassurance. The point is that they know you're still around, looking after them and not cross, but your visits aren't giving them enough attention to be worth waiting all that time for. Sooner or later they'll realise that the fuss simply isn't worth making.

- The same routine works if your child repeatedly wakes in the night. Leave them for five minutes, then briefly reassure them and leave for 10 minutes next time, and so on.

- If your child is prone to get out of bed, either at bedtime or in the night, take them back to bed and use the same words every time, for instance, 'It's time to sleep now'. Tuck them in and leave the room. Use this pattern over and over if necessary until they stay in bed and fall asleep. If you can stick with it, it will work.

- Although this approach can feel cruel and overly tough at

times, it does generally work within a few nights. Remember this is all about your child exploring boundaries, and there are always times when what they need to do will result in tears. However, if you offer reassurance and remain consistent toddlers not only learn with this technique, but also all the family is rewarded with a proper night's sleep.

However, if you don't feel this technique is right for you, or if you can't bring yourself to do it, this next method takes longer, but has good results.

It operates on the sound principle that children develop specific and necessary 'cues' within their normal sleep routine to fall asleep. For example they may only be able to go to sleep if they are lying next to you, or twiddling your hair, or being cuddled (and yes, we all know you shouldn't have got yourself into this mess of cues in the first place, but most of us do). This may apply at bedtime only, or may also apply every time they wake in the night. (Even as adults most of us can't fall asleep unless we're lying in a particular position, lying on our favourite side of the bed, or some other routine.) Your child needs to learn a different set of cues which enable them to go to sleep on their own.

- If your child is used to you lying next to them while they fall asleep, instead of lying simply sit next to them touching them.

- Once your child falls asleep easily in this way, sit next to the bed without touching them.

- Once this has become routine, move the chair a little way from the bed.

- Eventually, in this way, you'll end up outside the door.

The following is an alternative strategy for putting an end to night waking:

- Set a much later sleep time, such as 10.30pm, and stick to it until your child is sleeping through the night. To achieve this you mustn't let your child nap at all during the day (this is the downside of this approach, as both of you will get very tired and stroppy).

- Wake your child at the usual time in the morning – don't allow them to sleep in. Sooner or later they're bound to sleep through the night because they'll be so exhausted.

- Once this happens, gradually bring forward the time they go to bed: about 15 minutes earlier for a couple of nights, then 15 minutes earlier again, and so on, until you have their bedtime back to a sensible time. This method is very tough but has a great rate of success for those parents desperate enough to do it.

9TH JUNE

Today I trapped a bee and threw it out of the house.

The only reason I dealt with this is because I was worried about my toddler. I don't like stinging flying things, and my fears are not helped by the Emperor calling everything a lady-bird and trying to pick it up.

It's only a little thing, but it made me start thinking about the boundaries we push, the extra lengths we go, because of our children. It started when he was a tiny baby and I used to get up in the night because he was crying, and I was so tired I could hardly see, but I needed to know he was OK.

In so many ways I have found such strength and bravery for so many things that I could never have summoned for myself, but I can for the Emperor.

12TH JUNE

My birthday party. Today I learned all parties are parties for the Emperor.

13TH JUNE

My birthday. I am an emotional wreck as people give me presents and are nice to me.

I make myself become accustomed to reading on my friends' live journals and blogs how wonderful the Emperor was at my party, rather than how wonderful the party was. I'm even beginning to accept that despite allocating him to another's care I cannot chill out and relax as he pretends to nose dive into furniture or run into fires. (He didn't do either; I'm convinced he was only torturing me for not paying him enough attention.)

15TH JUNE

This morning I am bleary eyed, having sat up to 3am preparing papers for the post. In preparation for what I knew was going to be a long night, the Emperor stayed up until the ridiculous time of 11pm. He is now (at 9am) awake, having breakfast and seeking fun.

And I have realised that it's not just this morning, but really quite often my first thought on waking is when can I reasonably expect him to go back to sleep?

Just as I am haunted by the ghost of Emily Pankhurst and driven to the polls every election day (even when I feel there is little point), so an army of 1950s mothers (in polka dot dresses) mentally upbraids me every time I leave the Emperor alone in his room.

And what is this doing to me? Apart from obviously driving me scatty, it also means I am becoming increasingly uninspired in the Emperor's company. He asks for amusement and I look blank, until he tells me what to do. (He is unfortunately rather good at commanding.) I'm sure this is good for his imagination, but it's not good for my mental well-being.

BURNOUT

This section is dedicated to all those times of burnout, when it's not that you're cross with your little one, but you are becoming increasingly mentally numb. It's those days when you wake and think how long will he sleep? When is my partner back to help? (How do single parents stay sane? They deserve awards, ticker tape parades and statues.)

It is also a reminder that if your child is fortunate enough to have a safe space to play, toys, and is clean and fed, then it is alright to give yourself a time-out for a while. As long as you answer any calls, fetch the child if he is unhappy or needs anything, then solitary play is when some very constructive learning and imagination building can be done. It is actually good for a child to work things out on their own and discover their own level of independence as long as they know you are there and ready to come to their aid in a time of need. Honestly. Trust me, I'm a mother too.

17TH JUNE

The end of an era. This morning I was working upstairs on the laptop, while the Emperor played downstairs with his HappyLand set. Suddenly it became clear all was not joyous in his realm, when the air was split by a horrendous cry. Upon rushing down the stairs I found a small toddler crying in the middle of the hall and a babygate still securely locked.

He was standing, rubbing his crown, so my immediate fears were slightly dispelled. He had climbed over and toppled. Of course, I felt incredibly guilty. The searing guilt any parent feels when they weren't there to catch was garnished with the horror of realising the babygate is a thing of the past. I phoned Dada with the terrible news, and he reckons we can add a piece of wood to raise the gate by the requisite inches, but I know he's only buying us a short space of time.

21ST JUNE

I am now more clearly defining my time between play and work. I can't help but feel that being interrupted every 10 minutes to give someone a plane ride on the swivel chair is generally going to lower the standard of my writing.

THE CUNNINGNESS OF TODDLERS

I need to mention somewhere the cunningness of toddlers, from the sneaky spoonful of dairylea cheese that is snuck past my peripheral vision while I'm typing and into my tea, to the grabbing of keys and shoving them in locks.

Toddlers are incredible mimics, but without the sense. I once locked my mother in the dining room when I was very little, and

---

97

she had her karmic revenge when the Emperor tried to lock me in the garden last week.

But the implications for safety are vast. Your toddler can unlock the front door mortise if they can reach and have the key. They will learn how to unlock simple window locks and car doors, and they will shove things in the video, CD and DVD drives. Do not underestimate them.

Every day you are shadowed by a very, very cunning, pint sized impersonator.

23RD JUNE

This morning I have a cold and the Emperor is playing (age appropriate) computer games. There has been a remarkable shift in his awareness. He no longer makes the characters run towards the screen. He shows me how to use the controls and frequently says, "Want help, Mama!" when he gets to a tricky bit. He still can't figure out much of the game, but his growing intelligence is obvious.

CHANGES AND BOREDOM

Sometimes changes are subtle or sometimes like today you find your toddler explaining how to use a remote control to you. ("It's the red button, Mama" – and it is.) This year is one of remarkable development, when your baby finally changes from someone the cat could beat in a quiz to a questioning, information seeking autonomous being. It's incredibly important you provide them with a stimulating environment.

- Maximise active toys over passive ones to create quality play.

- Passive toys like TV do all the work for the child.

- Active toys encourage imagination, and can be used in a variety of ways and games.

- By this time children no longer need to be constantly amused, but are learning how to move from one activity to the next on their own.

- Active toy choices include cuddly animals, blocks, simple puzzles and books.

- Many toddlers love messy play such as water, sand, mud or leaves.

- Empty cardboard boxes provide hours of fun and can be anything from a space rocket to a fairytale castle.

28TH JUNE

Yay! We are getting verbs; verbs and sentences. After climbing on my desk chair spinning, and not surprisingly falling off, banging his head and crying, the Emperor said, "Dada, make it better!" I'm sure I'll be just as proud of him when he finishes his first brain surgery.

1ST JULY

Food isn't going well. A friend reduced me to hysterical laughter merely by asking which vegetables the Emperor prefers. There has been a slight movement in tastes. He will now eat wholemeal crackers and hummus. Cheese spread is sometimes acceptable, but never cheese. He runs shrieking from fruit and the sight of a boiled potato brings on a furious round of

"No. No. No. No. No. No," making him sound like a baby Gatling gun. He also likes salsa.

Why this strange mixture, you may be asking. Don't they feed their baby normal food? We do. We also allow him to pick bits and pieces off our plates, having long ago sorrowfully abandoned the concept of us all eating the same thing. (This mainly because I could no longer look an Oxfam commercial in the face considering the amount of food he was wasting each week.)

My Canterbury granny tells me her granddaughter (two and a half) achieved a red letter day recently by being seen to devour an inch and a half of grilled bacon. Despite her unwillingness to eat at all she has passed all her health visitor exams with flying colours.

TODDLERS' CHOICE

Generally toddlers know what they need to eat. Many of them are not adventurous with food. You do need to monitor their diet for necessary proteins and vitamins, but it's surprising how much they can get from fruit juice, rusks, milk, cheese and bread.

The one exception to toddlers knowing what they want is that many, like the Emperor, would eat chocolate until they bust. Sweeties don't come under the general rule.

- Continue to offer a variety of food. Beans that are hated one month may be loved the next. But do try to include one thing you know they will like.

- Never force a toddler to eat.

- Never leave a child hungry. If they won't eat their greens then give them something else, but keep it simple.

- Don't allow complaining about food. Make it a rule you can say no, but cannot complain about it.

- Don't extend mealtimes unduly.

- When you are eating together offer food from your own plate. Not only does this save waste, but for some reason parental food is always intriguing.

- Do try to find a fruit your child will eat. Textures make a difference to a lot of children – squishy bananas or crunchy apples can become firm favourites.

- Try the 'you can have' approach, as in "You can have the chocolate after you've finished the banana."

- Most food fads fade. Don't talk about a child's eating habits in front of them outside of meal times. (Don't make a fuss!)

- Being at nursery or playgroup helps. Toddlers are programmed by nature to be inquisitive and seeing others, especially other children, try out foods is the best way to widen their diet.

5TH JULY

Today the local surgery was offering a free sunhat and sunscreen, so we went along to get a goodie bag. The day was being organised by a Macmillan Nurse who, seeing the Emperor, uttered the appropriate words, "Isn't he lovely!" Which he is, but he likes to be acknowledged. After such a promising start I took the opportunity to ask her what I should say to parents reading this book – and together we came up with EFP.

CANCER PROTECTION FOR TODDLERS

It might seem ridiculous to think about this, but good habits set up now will be kept in later life, and if we've learnt anything from modern medicine, it's that prevention is better than cure. For the best protection against cancer:

E – Exercise Anything and everything, from swimming to running and playing. Discourage your toddler from being a couch potato.

F – Fruit By now we all know toddlers are faddy eaters, but you need to keep presenting fruit to them until you find one they like.

P – Protection Keep children out of direct sunlight between 11am and 3pm. Toddlers need a sun cream with a protection factor of 30. Spot test new creams. If your child wears a t-shirt while swimming to help protect against sunlight when they come out of the water they need to change to a dry one. A drying t-shirt is an ineffective sunshield. And hats – toddlers and young children need hats.

That's your basic EFP.

7ᵀᴴ JULY

So today I'm reading a report on the BBC News site about how it's wrong to raise little boys as tough when the Emperor summons me to display his newly invented toy. He has placed a HappyLand plastic person in a sock, so when he swings it at things it makes a resounding thwack.

Yes, the Emperor has created a cosh. Some little boys obviously don't need any encouragement to become tiny warriors. Nursery school is going to be such fun.

9TH JULY

THE POLITICAL PARENT

As a parent I've certainly thought about my world view, values and what I want my child to learn, but I find myself almost daily considering how child rearing is perceived and performed in this country.

Should parents be given a parental leave allowance? Would this help child delinquency? Would it encourage younger mothers? Would it open the door to allowing the government more say over how children are raised? Why should the childless have to pay for other people's children?

I love the Emperor. I will care for him regardless of whether the government decides to pay me for it. I will put him into nursery part time when he is three for both our sakes. I will somehow find the money to pay the extra all nurseries ask, as simply using the government hours is unacceptable to all our local nurseries, who will not take a child for only $2^1/2$ hours a day.

Why should someone pay towards child allowances when they have no children? Simply because they choose to be part of society, and society needs continuity. Children are not luxuries or expensive toys; they are necessary to the continuation of the human race. Helping the next generation grow is an amazing opportunity, but it seems is barely valued by a western world that wants fun, freedom and entertainment without responsibility.

10TH JULY

I've been reading over some of my previous entries, and for a professional writer there were a lot of spelling and grammatical mistakes. Sometimes I forget how exhausting spending all day with my toddler is until I see the results in my work.

And at night I get so tired I dream of sleep.

13ᵀᴴ JULY

On Saturday the Emperor did two amazing things. (He's also been so active since that I simply haven't had a chance to sit down and write. My inbox is full of unanswered emails and my answering machine is blinking desperately.)

The first thing was that he went for his first swimming lesson. All the toddlers took an adult with them into the pool for comfort, and there were times when the super-confident Emperor was clinging to his Dada for dear life.

SWIMMING LESSONS

The two most important things toddlers learn in early swimming lessons are:

- Confidence. Learning to swim can turn into an overwhelming experience. Swimming pools are noisy, busy places. An early approach will make learning to swim a smooth transition.

- Safety. One of the first things the tots in the Emperor's class learn is to make their way to the side of the pool and hold on. The thinking is if they ever fall into a pond or a stream they will know exactly what to do.

Parent and Child classes are a wonderful idea. If, like my son, your child is not potty trained you can buy swimmers' nappies. (It's worth noting here that a few doctors express concern over the potential severe health risks to all pool users when using

---

these.) Most classes will use flotation devices like armbands, so buying your own early on will allow you both to go swimming together in between classes.

I have mixed feelings about armbands, because it is very difficult to learn to swim while wearing them. They are really used for safety reasons and for building confidence. However, you do have to ensure the child is given opportunities out of bands to learn how to kick properly and start arm movements.

Things you can do to encourage swimming

- Use a lifeguard monitored swimming pool, not the sea.

- Always be in the pool with them. If you're not a good swimmer then this may be the time for relatives to step forward to help while you learn to swim too.

- Stay within an area where you can stand up easily. Treading water and dealing with a scared child is not a good combination.

- Encourage your child to put their face in the water and blow bubbles. (Many children have an aversion to putting their faces and mouths in the water.)

- Move a couple of steps away from the poolside and practise swishing your child forward without armbands, and then let go when you push. Do not do this until your child has learned how to cling onto the side confidently, and be ready to catch them if they struggle. Alternatively do this between two adults.

- Try to make swimming part of your regular schedule.

- Be aware children get cold and tired very quickly. One minute they are splashing around happy as a lark and the next they are shivering and snivelling. Start with 15 minute sessions and build up the time each week.

- Swimming is tiring. Have juice and a snack on hand for afterwards, or treat them in the pool café.

And then to make the day complete we took the Emperor to the cinema, where he did his second amazing thing and behaved perfectly.

TOP TIPS ON TAKING YOUR CHILD TO THE CINEMA

- U-rated films are rated for four and up, but cinemas generally allow you to take in younger children. Some cinemas only let young children in before 5pm or 6pm, so check before you go.

- A good gauge of whether your child is ready to see a movie is how long they will pay attention to a movie at home. A cinema movie is more enthralling, bigger, brighter, and in the dark, so don't worry if they get a bit restless with a home show, as long as they will sit for three quarters of a DVD at home, they're probably ready for the big screen.

- Do know all about the film you are going to see. My son loved Shrek 2 because it was bright, colourful, fast paced and followed on from Shrek, which he had seen at home. At the same time the cinema was also showing a U-rated film about the tribesmen of the Gobi desert. (This is a wonderful film, but would bore any toddler to tears.)

- Get a booster seat. (Most cinemas will have stacks of these in the lobby, but occasionally you need to ask.)

- If you have a toilet trained child sit near an aisle.

- Snacks and a drink are essential.

- Let them take a favourite cuddly toy. Even the most child friendly films can be a bit intimidating the first time.

- Be prepared that you may have to leave. If you do have to make a quick exit don't make a big deal of this. As usual, take things easy with the toddler, go with the flow and don't invest in trouble for the future.

17ᵀᴴ JULY

Today was one of those awful Saturdays when, despite the best of plans, I found myself so short of food I had to head to the supermarket. I'm lucky. I hate supermarkets, but the Emperor loves them. He know if he is good for the whole hour he will get a treat.

When we got there, I managed to get a parent and child space, excellent ideas that they are. They're near the shop to save you having to trail your child through cars, and have extra wide spaces for getting your child in and out of their car seat, and setting up your buggy. Of course there are never enough, but that doesn't excuse what I saw today; a child no more than 30 months old wandering after its father through parked cars and across busy lanes. The father was pushing a trolley, which had an empty baby seat. And he wasn't the only one.

I don't know if it's a local way of culling the population, but it's a prevalent issue in my city.

SAFETY IN CAR PARKS

Strap your toddler in a buggy. Or better yet pick them up and carry them in car parks; buggies aren't easy for drivers to see either. Even older children need their hands held while they are still developing their road sense. Cars in car parks move slowly, but they hit hard, especially when you're tiny. And of course, if you're driving, take extra, extra care in a car park, and in any areas where children may be moving between cars. (This includes your own driveway. The number of children who are hit every year by their parents reversing out is horrific.)

- If you have a runaway type toddler use a child harness.

- Don't allow your toddler to tease you about running or turn it into a game. Take them firmly by the hand and seriously tell them not to pull away again.

- Don't ever let running around near roads, car parks or in big shops become a game.

20TH JULY

Sometimes I feel like screaming too.

I've just had another tussle with the Emperor about changing his nappy. This was complete with crying, screaming, throwing himself to the ground and banging his head off whatever was near by.

What was all this about?

He didn't want to be told what to do, and I'd been working this afternoon. I stop whenever he asks for anything, and he has plenty to play with and is generally good at amusing himself. But whenever I ask him to do this, I pay for it later. So here I am, my head half fried from writing, dealing with an angry little boy who thinks if I won't pay him attention every minute of the day then he can damn well do as he pleases. My sole consolation at this point is that it is only three hours to bedtime, and some of that time will be taken up with a bath.

I understand why he is upset. I don't blame him at all. But no matter what you do, be it sitting at your laptop or hoovering your house, there will be times when your toddler does not have your undivided attention, and they will hate it.

ATTENTION

Both parents and children have to acclimatise to children not receiving full on attention all the time. Of course you have to ensure their environment is safe. Of course it's not OK to ignore your child by plonking them in front of the telly all the time. But the hard fact of toddlerhood is that there will always be times when they want more attention than you can feasibly give. The optimum way of seeing this is to be flattered: flattered that the little one wants you so much. The optimum way to deal with tantrums resulting from a perceived lack of attention is with humour and kindness. You can't scold a child for wanting more of their parents' time.

(And while I was writing this, the Emperor emptied the whole of his juice cup over the coffee table to play splashy-splashy.)

- In a safe environment (like their bedroom or playroom), with you nearby, a toddler can be left to play as long as they are happy to do so. (But we're talking about playing with toys here, not watching the telly.)

- Occasionally show that you've noticed what your child is doing when he's playing alone with comments such as, "You've used lots of red bricks," or "I see you've got the zoo animals and the horses."

21ST JULY

This morning the Emperor was talking of forests and the lady who did magic in the woods. This afternoon he was constructing a play with some of his toys with me taking some parts, but most of the action being supplied by the imperial director. I lay this firmly at the door of his father's choice of bedtime reading. They've just finished The Hobbit and it is doing him the world of good.

BOOKS

Toddlers love stories that are simple and bright. Yes, you may know by heart who Maisy Mouse picks up on her bus, but the simple repetition is exactly what helps toddlers learn. These are the kind of books that will encourage necessary language skills and word recognition.

- Books that name lots of everyday objects help with vocabulary.

- Pop-up and flap books are particularly engaging, especially if they are in large format.

- Generally toddlers have short attention spans, so short straightforward stories are good.

- At bedtime children may be happy to listen to more complicated tales. Even if they don't understand every word all toddlers love the sound of their parents' voices and the one to one attention that comes with being read to.

- It's a nice idea to let the parent who sees the child least (for work or whatever reason) read the bedtime stories.

- Local libraries encourage children to borrow books, and would

---

> much prefer books to be returned a bit dog-eared than not borrowed at all.

23RD JULY

Yesterday the Emperor fell down the stairs. He darted ahead of me, took four steps very quickly in his rush to get outside, and then tumbled, like the best of stunt men, down the rest of the steep flight. Time slowed. Half way down I saw his agonised face, and his deep blue eyes cast me a "Mama, why aren't you saving me" look?

I don't think I can find the words to express how awful this was.

But he's fine. Not even a bruise. As soon as he hit the bottom he was on his feet and demanding hugs. Five minutes later he was trying to open the front door and get out. In the play park he attempted to throw himself off the edge of the slide with his normal joyous abandon.

His mother isn't faring so well. The guilt is now merely a red, raw, stabbing pain and the shaking and the desire to burst into tears has subsided to a controllable level. His father, who I phoned at once, took it in his stride. "He's old enough to tell you if there is anything wrong," he said. "And you've checked for any signs of concussion. He's fine." He didn't even blame me. It was entirely my fault. No, the Emperor shouldn't have started down the stairs, but neither should I have taken my eyes off him for those few seconds when sunglasses seemed so important.

We do have a babygate but it's across the door upstairs, not the stairwell (there is no way to rig this thanks to the rickety nature of this old cottage). So once released I have to ensure

I am holding his hand or in front of the Emperor as he rushes for the outside world. I wasn't quick enough. I wasn't worried enough. I am so lucky.

AFTERMATH

Even when you think all is under control, your toddler can put on that burst of speed and surprise you. Finding the balance between smothering your toddler in protective padding and allowing them some independence is hard. It's likely there will be accidents even for the most safety conscious parents.

If you have any doubts at all about your child's well-being take them to the local surgery or the local A and E. My surgery, which I think is quite typical, is very happy for you to phone ahead and drop by with your accident victim in cases where you think they are OK but aren't quite sure. (Of course, if it's serious you're going to phone an ambulance.)

Toddlers are very good at telling you if they are hurt. Their cries change – often to silence. Above all, if they are leaping up immediately and running around, they're probably OK. Do have a child first aid book in the house, and do learn the signs of concussion. Toddlers bang their heads (as well as other bits) all the time. If you can manage a child first aid course, even better.

Do move on as quickly as possible after any problems. No matter how frightened you are, making a big deal out of an accident will only serve to upset the child more. The exception is where a child gets into difficulties through ignoring your instructions. This needs to be firmly explained as soon as they are calm and comforted enough to understand. Whatever has happened, reassurance has to come first. A frightened child is not helped by your anger or your fears.

Also, if you have a partner, or even a friend you can phone at the time for a brief two minute check, it can help place the situation in perspective. Having a back-up responsible adult who won't panic, but knows enough about childcare to ask the right questions, can make the difference between a parent going into full shock and just shaking a lot.

And may all your mishaps be as minor as mine.

29TH JULY

Along with a sudden and disconcerting desire to arrange train and car crashes among his toys, the Emperor has developed the Flop'n'drop. Sometimes the Flop'n'drop is preceded by a scream that vibrates my skull, and is often followed by a fit of banging his head on the floor until it is sore enough to make him stop and cry, while throwing me accusing looks. Causes of Flop'n'drop include the obvious: having to leave the play park, being told he needs a nap (when he is exhausted and falls asleep three minutes after being put in his room) and generally being requested to anything he does not wish to do. Less obvious causes include attempting to change his nappy (the Emperor remains too active to be interested in certain bodily functions) and being prevented from climbing the bookcases.

BOUNDARIES

It's worth reminding yourself that toddlers constantly push boundaries, and much of the behaviour at this time is transitory. Firm, consistent treatment is the only answer. Don't reward naughty behaviour; time-out in the bedroom is fine. Taking a break for a cup of tea is fine. Feeling very angry with your toddler is fine as long as your behaviour remains firm and consistent. If you display your temper to your toddler, he will feel he has every right to do the same to you. Remember you are the adult and, if necessary, sneak away to chew the furniture in private.

The tantrum rule

Do not rise to provocative behaviour. Even if your toddler gets angry attention through his misbehaviour he is still getting the attention he wants and redirecting you away from your original intent.

CRIES AND TANTRUMS

All children are different, but as an example the Emperor's cries fall into roughly six categories. In order of rising importance these are:

1 The Grizzle. A half-hearted cry that is punctuated by peeps from under his eyelashes or through his fingers. This is a test to see if a few tears will win him the day; the craftiest of the cries in his armoury.

2 The Shriek of Rage. This makes full use of all the octaves available to a small child, but which are denied to adults. If I lean over him when he is in full pelt I literally feel the bones in my skull vibrate. This is the pure rage cry of an Emperor not getting his own way.

3 The Wail. Mama, I'm unhappy. This is a desperate rising and lowering cry that also incorporates a very puppy like whine. He is unhappy and wants comfort.

4 The Bellow. A huge protest that the world isn't behaving the way he expected, for example gravity does not conform to his will. Not usually brought on by a tantrum, and usually preceded by...

5 The Big Intake. This is the sound of a gigantic intake of air and is followed by a Bellow. It happens when the Emperor falls out of bed, off his chair, or lands on his face when playing too enthusiastically. It is the sound of shock, but it is also a reassuring noise. The big bellow means physically he is OK.

6 Silence. Usually preceded by a thump. The real danger sign is silence. If a child falls and does not cry but sits silent, or seems woozy, then you are most likely in for a trip to A and E. The Emperor has had a couple of Big Intakes that for a heart-stopping minute mimicked Silence.

30TH JULY

Today is the first day I saw him set up a car track for a car and race it around obstacles without attempting to destroy anything. I think we have finally embarked on a stage that could be called constructive play.

7TH AUGUST

I have a plan. Today I received yet another generous tithe of gifts for the Emperor (a five piece musical set). It is both lovely and very loud. At current count we have one toy box, one toy chest, a huge six drawer thing (the drawers containing more than your average bucket), two portable plastic boxes, toys under the stairs, and toys generally strewn all around the house. Oh wait! I forgot the chest of bath toys.

It's too much.

Whichever set the Emperor wants to play with is always missing a bit, entailing exhausting and endless searches. More often than not these searches end only when I am on my knees

weeping, because I have failed my son and have not managed
to find the HappyLand Nurse that he has been insistently
demanding for the past three days, and for which I have
rescheduled my entire week to spend the morning in a fruit-
less search. It is then, and only then, that he will snake his tiny
hand behind, or underneath, some piece of furniture that I
had previously thought not even the cat could get her skinny
paw beneath, and pull out the small plastic figurine of a nurse
wielding a psychopathic grin. This is the point at which I
realise he doesn't actually need this blasted lump of moulded
plastic: he needed the applause he was sure would erupt when
he held his spoils triumphantly aloft and cried "Found it!" in
the same tones as Caesar must have surely used when claiming
Britain.

He is beginning to realise that this exercise doesn't seem to
get him the applause it did the first few times, and perhaps this
game is nearing its end.

For me it proves beyond a shadow of a doubt that toddlers,
despite what the stores will tell you, need attention far more
than they need toys.

I have therefore launched Operation Locate, Divide, Secure
and Rotate.

TOO MANY TOYS?

Modern toddlers are often the receivers of copious gifts and
presents. In a room littered with toys a toddler will transform in to
hummingbird before your eyes darting here, there and everywhere with boundless energy, rarely engaged with anything, and
at the end of the day rather like a call centre operator – strung out
and exhausted from too many claims on their attention.

- The first plan of attack: when someone asks what your little one would like for birthday/Christmas/etc be ready with an answer. You can be polite and say it's very nice of you, don't feel as if you need to… blah, blah, but give precise instructions as to what you want. If they ask, tell them – or you will end up, as a friend of mine did, with 300 pieces of pretend play food. (No toddler has that many teddies to feed.)

- Secondly, launch your own Operation Locate, Divide, Secure and Rotate (OLDSR). Sort out the toys into varying types and make up batches for daily use. Five to eight different toys or sets are way more generous than I should be, but that's what I aim for. All other toys should be secured out of sight. (Of course Stinky Bear or other beloved stuffies don't count in this batching, but perhaps if not Stinky Bear some of his legions of plushie friends who make up the Praetorian Guard might like to stay in bed/on the shelf?)

- Change the toys every few days so your toddler doesn't get bored, but has enough time to engage and explore what a particular toy is all about.

- Tidy. They will go through phases when all they want to do is draw or paint. Wonderful, put everything else away. It's great if you can encourage your toddler to clear up by using low toy boxes and storage bins, but realistically even if it's you putting everything in the box for now, your living environment is going to be clearer, safer and, let's face it, cleaner. (It is extremely difficult hoovering around a HappyLand citadel and farm complex without unleashing on the little plastic people and their livestock the kind of catastrophe that spun Toto and Dorothy into another world, and with a far less happy ending.)

- At the end of the day there won't be so much to put away. This means you should have both the energy and the time to

> create a toy free zone to relax in. However much you love your little one it is good to find some time when you don't feel as if you are living in a toy box.

10TH AUGUST

We're having one of those days. The Emperor was playing happily in his room, when someone left the house without saying goodbye to him. The wailing and screaming this caused had me pelting down the stairs like some Mama baby-seeking missile to check on him. He was in a terrible state, so I spent some time trying to calm him down. Every now and then a grin broke through the wails, and finally the storm passed. He began to play with toys on the floor. I got up to leave.

I imagine you've guessed the result; wails loud enough that the nearby shipping changed course. I asked him if he wanted to come to the living room with me, and again the answer was no. Finally it dawned on me he was not hungry, he was not thirsty, he did not need his nappy changed, he did not want to play with me. No, he wanted me to sit right next to his toy box like some extra large Mama-teddy. I left to the sound of rage filled sonic baby squeals.

Right now I want nothing more than to cuddle my loving little boy, but I know if I pander to these tantrums then I won't simply have a monstrous toddler, I will be laying the groundwork for a monstrous man. On the positive side if I can match wits with my little one I defy any recalcitrant adult to attempt to push me around.

REVIEW: THREE QUARTERS OF THE WAY THROUGH THE TERRIBLE TWOS

MY GOALS

1 By the time he is three the Emperor will be eating a healthy mixed diet without complaint, and pudding bribes will be a thing of the past.

   Still standing at 6/10.

2 Nappies will be a dim memory, with all bodily waste products going in the loo, without having to go through the hell of pottydom.

   I think with the bedroom protest we're actually going backwards. 1/10

3 Every night the Emperor will go down for at least 10 hours of undisturbed rest.

   Bedtimes remain too irregular. 7/10

4 As mother I will continually strive to provide entertainment and activities suitable for the Emperor's developing mind and body (which includes ethically correct selection of toys and television programs).

   He's now playing computer games and, while these are age appropriate, it's not exactly active play. 6/10

5 I will begin the socialisation process of the Emperor by finding him other children to play with, and cease surrounding him totally with servile adults.

   Still waiting for playgroup, but swimming and other play sessions ongoing. 6/10

6　At the end of the year, the Emperor will be able to give his real name and address when asked, and will be fluent in conversational adult-speak.

We have verbs and imaginative storytelling. 8/10

7　I will ensure that the Emperor's surroundings are safe, and that we never have another occurrence of the collapsed babygate and the stairs.

There isn't a mark low enough; he fell down the stairs. 0/10

8　I will undertake to school the Emperor in the ways of acceptable behaviour without resorting to corporal punishment, or anything that may entail long term therapy (for either of us) at a later date.

He has massive anger issues. Flop'n'drop, spitting and hitting are daily occurrences. But we are both working with these. 5/10

9. I will not work full time. I will devote huge amounts of each day to the caring of the Emperor and his environs, but I will also write, study and achieve a minimal level of social life.

As if. 5/10

10 I will not be a sucker for the Emperor's huge blue topaz eyes or other formidable weapons in his armoury of manipulation and cajolement.

As if. 4/10

THE EMPEROR'S GOAL

1　To bend the known universe to his will.

We're drawing level. 5.5/10

11ᵀᴴ AUGUST

I have just been to see my GP, where I surprised myself by becoming quite tearful during the consultation. I'd noticed for some time I had been sleeping badly, and that my concentration when playing with the Emperor was not good. After a discussion in which I described my average day we came to the conclusion that I have entered a phase of too intensive mothering, and that I need to start spending time away from the Emperor to prepare us both for the transition of him entering nursery in the New Year.

I often feel I am not a good enough mother and this is, I know, a very common feeling. I expect that sometimes I will feel bored doing the things a two year old wants to do. How many times can you pretend utter delight that a little car will run down a toy ramp? But we've gone beyond that stage to where I am mentally starving, and yet still focusing completely on the Emperor.

What my GP told me, and which surprised me, is that this is not the required state of affairs for a mother with a toddler.

I am still thinking about how to accomplish change.

BALANCE

Being the parent of a small child is hard.

Remaining yourself while being the parent and full time carer of a small child is even harder. It is OK to want to have fun that isn't directly related to parenting activities.

As parent and child approach the big three, they both need space apart. While current research is suggesting spending more time with someone who thinks you are the best person in

---

the world is good for two years and under, by the time a child reaches three they not only need to mix with their peers, but with adults who relate to them in a way other than as doting parents.

12ᵀᴴ AUGUST

In the spirit of finding more quality time for the Emperor and I apart, I finally got back to phoning around nurseries. The Emperor won't go until January, and he will be going part time; the main purpose of this (apart from saving my sanity) is to allow him to socialise with his peers.

I know this isn't starting the separation plan for the Emperor and me, but at least for me it's a step on the way. I need to find some affordable day classes for him now.

13ᵀᴴ AUGUST

Yet another box that is inscribed with the mystic symbol 36mths+. As I watch him play I wonder how this grand epiphany will seize him. On the 10th of November I am expecting no less than a roll of celestial drums, the darkening clouds to part, and a shaft of heaven sent illumination to descend upon the Emperor, whereupon he will be filled with all the knowledge and wisdom of three years. There is no other way to explain this. According to toy manufacturers worldwide he will be able to manage so many things.

The reality is he is currently advanced enough to enjoy some of the 36months+ toys – especially the puzzles and shape orientated ones – and that at 36 months he may still not have the sense to refrain from eating the small indigestible parts of a pirate.

AGE LIMITS – THE MYTH OF 36MTHS+

Age limits for toys, puzzles and clothes can only ever be a guide. There is a big change in both the kind and the number of toys available for the three year old. Age labels mean this is suitable for the average child, and as all of us know our own children are certainly not average. (Whoever heard of an average Emperor?) In particular the 'unsuitable for 0-3 years' mark is due to the size of small items and whether or not they could be inhaled by a young child liable to put things in their mouth.

- Guidelines are useful but not sacrosanct. The wisest course of action is to examine any new toy before you give it to a child. Obvious hazards are strangling (with wires, cords or strings) and choking (on small components, which includes batteries, which should be behind the kind of panels that screw in rather than clip).

- Depending on your child's strength and forcefulness of play, you also need to think about what they can break and whether sharp edges or shards will occur.

- Toys for toddlers should also be washable.

- Check batteries; the Emperor was once given a very nice toy that had cheap batteries in it which leaked.

- Always choose toys with a safety kite mark. British and European trading standards have caused a huge improvement in toy safety.

- If you decide to give your child a toy that is supposedly for an older child you need to be very cautious and supervise their play. Also, unless you do have a toddler who is bathed in a white and enlightening celestial ray please don't assume just

> because they are 36mths+ that the toy will be right and safe
> for them.

17ᵀᴴ AUGUST

Spurred on mainly by guilt I went to see another nursery today. The Emperor's father felt I should have ironed his (the Emperor's) clothes to create a good impression; I didn't want to raise unrealistic expectations in the staff. We walked through the park to a lovely nursery, where we were greeted by friendly staff, who were somewhat overwhelmed by 11 new children joining their nursery that day. It wasn't the best time to catch them, but I had phoned ahead. Overall there was an atmosphere of controlled panic. One little boy was placed behind me in an upright chair with a snack and then ignored. He watched the room with wide, sad eyes. In the corner four little three year old girls played and screamed, with no one seeming to watch them. The owner was very understanding of my reluctance to send the Emperor to nursery, but she didn't instil in me any confidence that she could handle the situation.

When I asked about multicultural festivals I was assured they'd done one recently this summer. When questioned more closely the nursery staff said they thought it was probably a Jewish one. At this point I began to seriously wonder about their organisational abilities.

I know the nursery is fully approved. I know that it is acceptable (though not ideal) to allow children to sleep in their buggies. I know there is nothing technically wrong with this nursery, but it didn't feel right in any way.

I have recorded the recent TV program on undercover investigation of nurseries, and in the interests of research I need to watch this. I didn't before this trip, because having worked in the media I know a good story is one that grabs you by the emotional short and curlies. It is unrealistic to imagine all nurseries in Britain run well when the inspectors are gone. And even, like today, when you see a nursery that does everything by the book, it can still not feel right.

As well as asking all the questions I cited in the earlier panel you need to find somewhere you can trust, but also trust your intuition about what feels right for your family.

25TH AUGUST

We've finally taken the last rail off the Emperor's conversion cot, and it's a proper little bed at last. Dada and I moved everything around in the room, and even managed to get most of the various bits and pieces of games and sets back together. The bed now faces out into the centre of the room, and it is a little boy's room rather than a baby's. The Emperor ran around delightedly. He has his very own space to play, with his desk, his toy box, and pop-up castle/tent.

MAKING A SPACE

Around this age children begin to relish their own space. A safe environment for them to play, arrange their own toys as they please, but still know you are nearby is a good step in preparing them for going to nursery. If they are sharing a room, making them their own corner is a good compromise.

Independent space encourages imaginative play. Finding the line between consigning your toddler to his room and giving him

---

space is a hard one to draw. I was feeling bad about leaving him in his room until one morning he threw a tantrum demanding his room. He invites me to play sometimes, and he knows I will always come when he calls, but largely he wants the space to himself, and I let him play there for a couple of hours a day.

27TH AUGUST

Every day more tantrums. This is so exhausting.

30TH AUGUST

Not a bank holiday in this house. I finally gave in and phoned the local helpline for nursery, nursery school and playgroup advice, all of which may be in partnership with the council, offer funded places, be inspected by HMI and teach the pre-school curriculum. The nice lady is sending me many lists, although she cannot tell me if anywhere actually has any places. I will have to visit them all myself.

The Imperial father has expressed concern that should the Emperor attend a nursery class at a primary school he might mix with primary school children and learn bad words a couple of years ahead of normal schedule. It had not occurred to me to worry about this. Only last week I was walking along the seafront when I passed a group of tots and their nursery nurses only to hear the adults speaking in what can best be described as colourful colloquial language.

However, as none of the tots was wearing 'We go to x nursery school badges' I don't even know which one to avoid. The nice lady on the phone suggested any place inspected by HMI must be wonderful. Even I remember how my teachers would suddenly transform themselves into lucid, intelligent and witty educators whenever there was an inspector in the room unlike their normal dull and moribund selves.

8TH SEPTEMBER

We have just returned from the play park, and I am writing this to the accompaniment of wails, screams and floor beatings from my toddler son. I have yet again succumbed to believing my mothering was inadequate because of 'stuff wot other people had writ'. This isn't to rubbish all psychology books out there. There are some excellent ideas on child raising and dealing with toddlers, but there is also a lot of guff, and while it may be true that children's reason makes huge steps forwards between two and three, the rate of progress varies from child to child.

WHAT I LEARNT FROM TODAY'S TANTRUM

- When you carry a squalling toddler home people stare at you as if you are a child beater. However, if the only other option is to allow your toddler to beat his head off the pavement in rage because you have to leave, you do what is right for your child and not what looks better. I could have patiently got down on my hands and knees, attempted to distract him and given him more time. This would have produced nothing more than a large bruise on his forehead. I could also have let him go back into the park, choosing to either stay there until he fell asleep or leaving later with an even greater tantrum and giving him the message that tantrums work.

- My son is pushing boundaries with me. He wants me to do everything his way and, while I will discuss options with him, a

---

tantrum means he loses all privileges. (Increasingly often now discussion is forestalling tantrums.)

- I will not be angry with my son for having a tantrum. I understand it comes from frustration. I also have times when life, people and the world in general frustrate me to the extent I want to scream and beat my fists on the floor, but as an adult I am not allowed to do this. I have to teach my son he too has to control his rage. When he is slightly older I will explain that by not giving into rage we can think our way out of frustrating circumstances from how to turn the block to fit in the puzzle, to how to outwit any would-be Machiavellians who cross our paths.

- During a tantrum I will speak sternly and clearly. I will stay near him if it seems to be helping but, despite what the newspapers were saying today, if I feel he is better able to calm himself alone, I will move out of his eyesight.

- I will also send him to nursery so he can learn how to interact with other children without forcing his way into their games or treating them as he does the cats. (The Emperor can be very sweet and kind, but he can also suddenly decide it is his slide and try to kick someone away by planting a foot in their face.)

- No matter how little I wish to let him go I need him to become more socialised.

One of the most frightening aspects of today's outing was when two six/seven year olds decided the Emperor had intruded into their game, ganged up on him to tickle him, and then one of them punched him in the back. It is one of my deepest fears that older children will hurt the Emperor. When he is older he will have to deal with bullies at school, but now at two he seems so vulnerable. The nursery attendants who were with these children acted quickly to ensure the boy apologised to the Emperor, who said without prompting, "That's all wight" and went on about his play. I, on the other hand, was trembling. My son was being playful and trusting. Sometimes he crosses boundaries but there is no menace intended. These older boys were learning the power of intimidation.

9TH SEPTEMBER

We're just back from a toddler gym class and my little angel is relaxing with juice and watching a Maisy video. I am exhausted, nursing two bites, a bruised ego and a deep sense of shame that I have somehow raised a wild animal rather than a child.

We arrived early, and the Emperor was very excited to see all the mats and equipment being put out. However, he behaved beautifully sitting with me and waiting for the lesson to begin. He met other children while we were waiting, and although he showed no understanding of why he couldn't just run up and hug someone, he was nice, gentle and even retrieved some toys for a little boy when he lost them. The class was intended for 18 months to three years old, and I watched with deep misgiving as one angelic tot after another arrived. Finally one little boy around the same age turned up.

Then the children were let onto the mats for songs and warm up before playing on the equipment. I seriously doubt the wisdom of allowing children to see fun things and then demand they do nursery rhyme songs, almost as much as I scorn the concept of giving some children large wooden sticks to drum on the floor, their knees and anyone who gets close enough. The Emperor was not impressed that he was prevented from flailing around for maximum noise and impact. But this was to be nothing compared to the rampaging gorilla he turned into once they were unleashed on the equipment.

He tried to force other children out of the way, ignored everything he was told and frequently had be mama-handled to avoid nasty accidents. Prior to this I had had one occasion of having to use the Mama of Doom voice to control him, and had been given evil looks by several parents who only spoke to their little one in syrupy whispers. However, when he was barrelling along at mach 4 in imminent danger of collision with their little darling their attitude towards the Mama of Doom voice changed, and they seemed to think it was a very good thing indeed.

The only child he showed any respect was a little Downs girl towards whom he was incredibly gentle and more than once tried to demonstrate equipment for her. And then, of course, came the end of the class, when the children are meant to march off neatly to collect their socks and shoes. This was bite one, but I managed to wedge him in a corner between some equipment to get his shoes on and, despite doing the stamp-snot-flop drill, I got him downstairs and out the door. He then demanded ice cream for good behaviour. He did not get it.

I don't think he is a bad child. Apart from biting me (which is bad but not as bad as him biting other children) I know his behaviour was all down to overexcitement and fury at the ending of a treat. This is not an excuse, but it leaves me somewhat at a loss to know how to deal with it. Obviously the more he socialises the better he will behave, but these current storms of fury are not the best way for a young Emperor to encourage his mother to be more adventurous with him.

WILD CHILDREN

I posted the above entry to my Internet diary, which a number of other mothers are watching, and received a flurry of heartfelt thanks that I admitted to having a wild child. Parents we meet are very good at telling you how wonderful their child is; they rarely tell you about the bad times.

All two year olds are different, and for some of them the twos is a very, very testing time. Other mothers may have perfect angels, but you may not, and no matter how much you, or I, are prone to self-blame, the truth is that some children are wilder than others.

12TH SEPTEMBER

The Emperor is drinking very competently from a cup. I admit he does call everything he drinks out of it 'tea', but this seems a small price to pay. He appears to have learnt from observing me drinking (you've guessed it) tea. The cups I bought for him ages ago, and which we tried and failed to get him to use, are now in constant demand. It really was as simple as that. Yesterday he said, "Want tea. Want cup." And when he was handed one, showed complete understanding of its use and purpose. He does have a tendency to occasionally stick his hand in and suck his fingers, but we think he learnt this from the cat, who often attempts to steal from teacups foolish people have placed on the floor. However, the Emperor can also use his lips properly on the cup's lip and so in this, as in many other ways, he is surpassing the cats.

IN THEIR OWN TIME

The number of things that I have fretted about the Emperor not managing has been endless. I'm not happy with what he is eating, but he is very healthy (far healthier than I as I sit here snuffling through a cold. The Emperor disdains colds.) I recall being terrified he would never speak. Now take him into any playground and he will be the most talkative child there. I used to worry he couldn't figure out puzzles designed in his age range whereas now his reverse engineering skills are financially formidable.

All in all the many things I feared he would never achieve have come to pass. I honestly believe toddlers have their own built in progress rate. Encouragement may make the gaining of skills a pleasanter activity, but like my Emperor they go at their own pace.

The moral of this panel is don't worry. There are guidelines for children's achievements at all ages, but this is exactly what they are: guidelines. A child isn't a project or a product, and will not conform to parental deadlines. In setting these all you do is gain yourself more grey hair.

The drinking from a cup may not seem a huge step forward (especially to childless friends), but for us it has been a significant reminder that in toddlerhood there is no rush. This is the most wonderful time of life (no mortgage, no exams, no washing to do, no money to earn, no responsibility) and while as a parent you must look on enviously, you can also share in the exhilarating excitement of your child exploring their new world; especially if you don't worry about the little things.

19TH SEPTEMBER

Today the Emperor visited the zoo for the second time, and this time he enjoyed it. It's remarkable to see the changes in his behaviour. Not only is he chatting away, he is also so much more aware of the surrounding world. Penguins are now the coolest things in the known Imperial world.

22ND SEPTEMBER

Red letter day. The Emperor is booked into nursery from January onwards for four half days, and the government is paying for the lot under their nursery scheme. My baby is growing up.

In the end I chose the granny staffed nursery, which has had a good press from everyone I have spoken to. It's a very, very small nursery. Children have to be taken to local play parks to have outside play. However, I haven't found any other nursery that feels as nice, as right and as welcoming. I don't need to choose between morning or evening sessions until mid-November, when I need to go in and sign the funding forms.

And of course because I have sorted this I get a phone call from the local playgroup, offering me a morning place for at least three days a week. I explain he is going to nursery next year and name the one I've chosen. "Oh," says the playgroup leader, "that's where my children go and it's lovely." I feel quite smug. She offers me a three morning slot for the Emperor, and says this can continue if he chooses to go to afternoon nursery. I ask if there is anything I need to be aware of and she says not really. However, when I point out he's not toilet trained yet, we have a problem. Apparently all 18 children (aged between two and a half and four) who attend each day are toilet trained. I find this a little difficult to believe. I also know I won't have toilet trained him by next Wednesday. The worker explains they will change the first poo and then call the parent to come down and change the second. This feels rather like both child and parent being penalised. I understand they are working on a tight budget and that changing children is a big deal, but I'm not happy about their solution. Especially as the playgroup hours are 9 to 11.30am and the Emperor's normal poo time is between 10 and 11am.

I will be interested to see how this all works. We're going along on Wednesday morning next week.

29TH SEPTEMBER

Today was the Emperor's first day at playgroup. There were not, as I had feared, toddlers flying like shrapnel as the Emperor assumed his rightful place as commander in chief of all playthings. Remarkably, he behaved extremely well, playing alone, joining other children at tables, and waiting his turn to paint. He refused to eat the poisonous apples and raisins at snack time, but happily poured milk all over himself. Generally he seemed to prefer the company of the girls, who were quite surprised. The boys were mostly older than him, and one in particular was a little more aggressive than the others. Later on, copying him, the Emperor rammed a little girl when they were all slalom racing outside. I fear I shall have to keep close tabs on who he associates with: it would be all too easy for him to turn to the dark side.

I am dubious if we will continue with this. I very much want my son to mix with other children, but towards the end of the morning the playworker opened the gate and my son ran straight past her into the road. I was not impressed. Earlier, the children had been playing on tricycles on their little tar-mac playground with no safety gear in sight. It's difficult to know if you're being overprotective. I witnessed at least two tussles in the playgroup, and was somewhat at a loss to know what to do. Am I allowed to pull other people's children apart? When I'm describing this to grandad he asks if parents who come in have any checks taken on them, and of course the answer is no. If you're a parent you're assumed to have never hurt or be capable of molesting a child. How do I feel about an adult I don't know taking my child to the toilet? What kind of a message am I giving telling him adults he doesn't know – and if it's the parent on duty rather than the play worker, an adult he may never have met before – are allowed to take down his trousers? The more I think about it, the unhappier I am.

30TH SEPTEMBER

What do you do? The Emperor was incredibly keen to go to playgroup this morning. So we go and I speak to the senior worker who says she understands my concerns and, worrying-ly, that they are as vigilant as they can be when they open the gate. (How, asks the Emperor's father afterwards, can that possibly be considered a good enough answer?)

I see her reaction as being defensive, maybe even slightly guilty and, like airlines, it seems to me playgroups are liable to be safer after one scare. The senior worker promises only she or the other permanent worker will take him to the toilet. She makes it sound as if it's down to his lack of toilet training. I don't care, she can play that however she wants as long as we get what he needs.

And then on the way out, having left the happiest little

Emperor ever, I realise I didn't hear the door click behind me. I turn round and go back through the open playground gate (open for parents to enter) and push on the door. Across a toddler crowded room my eyes meet those of the senior worker, who looks aghast when I ask coldly if this door is meant to be open. "Someone must have latched it," she says hurrying over to lock me out.

Are two scares going to make them a better playgroup or just an incompetent one?

8TH OCTOBER

Parent duty at the playgroup. I won't say the senior worker and I are best friends, but we seemed to have reached a truce. Of course this could all be in my mind. I realise I am being remarkably wary of people who get to care for my son, even more so than I expected.

My part of the day went well. I did more washing up than I have done for years and I successfully made 'snack' (a meal invented by nurseries and playgroups everywhere). I did my best to interact with the children, who found me a strange and frightening beast.

Sadly, the Emperor isn't a perfect angel child, as I saw today. While all the other little tots were sitting prettily on their chairs waiting for a story the Emperor was running round the room at mach 4 until he had to be ejected into the other room. Later, he spat in the faces of two girls. My only consolation is that he was not the child who hit another little girl over the head with the wooden rolling pin the children use for playdough.

ASK WHAT YOUR CHILD DOES

It was very useful to see what the Emperor got up to at play-group. Neither of the workers had previously mentioned his inability to sit still for a story, nor his spitting habit. Children behave differently away from their parents, although the foundations are laid at home. (How could I have known because he saw the cats hiss and spit at each other he would think it was fine to spit at little girls?) You cannot reprimand your child for responses like spitting when you aren't there. All playgroups and nurseries should have a document setting out how they deal with reprimands, which should be available for you to view. However, you can still talk to your child about their behaviour. You can also work on encouraging and reinforcing other areas. Talk to your playgroup leaders or nursery staff. It's all too easy in the excitement of collecting your tottering bundle of joy not to ask how they have been doing. Also ask explicit questions. Avoid merely seeking confirmation that your child behaved well; ask how he got on in different areas. How is he relating to other children? Does he eat his snack? Does he sit quietly when asked? What does he seem particularly interested in doing? What does he avoid?

12TH OCTOBER

I felt a great deal of shame the first time my cat was sick over a guest, but this was nothing compared to my feelings when I picked up the Emperor from playgroup today. He had hit another child over the head causing a minor head wound, which had bled copiously. He had then followed this up by spitting in the face of a little girl who cried for half an hour.

The father of the child he hit was actually on parent duty, and was remarkably unconcerned about the whole thing. I was deeply impressed by his attitude. It would have been all too easy to be angry with the Emperor; possibly even as angry and disappointed as I was.

INCIDENTS AT PLAYGROUP

Toddlers aren't very good at explaining their side of the story. Nor are they very good at appreciating that they have upset or hurt another child. (This isn't their fault. It's an awareness that develops with age.)

Toddlers are very good at learning the boundaries of behaviour. Being in a social environment is very different from being at home, especially if you are an only child like the Emperor. (It's quite telling that the bad behaviour began in week two, only once he'd begun to settle in.)

Work with your playgroup leader and, while you need to be firm with your child, you also need to talk to them about what happened. If your child is capable of discussing what happened even better, but at two and a bit that can be a lot to ask.

- Toddlers may 'misremember' an incident to avoid punishment – and they may also not realise there is anything wrong with doing this.

- Deal with this by showing your child how they should behave: discipline, praise and set an example.

- Use the best evidence to decide what happened. If it appears the child did actually do what they are claiming they didn't, extend the normal time-out, and explain this is because they didn't tell you what really happened. Mention you are disappointed they didn't tell you the truth.

- If it's not clear what happened, unless it's a very serious incident, let it go – otherwise you risk training a creative fabricator.

- Praise your child when they do tell the truth, and avoid telling 'polite' lies around young children who won't be able to tell the difference (for example, don't tell Auntie Mavis in front of the toddler she doesn't look fat if she is clearly the width of a double decker bus).

That evening, to show my support for the playgroup, I went along to their committee meeting and ended up being appointed co-chair (and I do have to fill in a form for security checks for this). There was a stunningly low attendance with most parents happy to drop their child off and leave them. This playgroup, like most, is a charity run by the parents themselves. There really is no excuse for parents not involving themselves in some way. If you want what is essentially cheap, safe care for your children in an environment that helps them learn to socialise then it seems to be only right that you get involved.

13TH OCTOBER

Hardly were the words, "We've had a good chat and I don't think you'll have any problem with hitting today", out of my mouth when the Emperor struck a little boy in the face with a toy knight. It was a very clear demonstration of 'This is my toy. I'm busy. Go away.'

I had a discussion with the group leaders, and I suggested that if he misbehaved again I remove him for the rest of the morning. I had just got home and made my cup of tea when the phone rang. After three incidents the playgroup needed me to pick him up. He was sitting with the senior playgroup worker playing happily. Within a few minutes of my being there he lashed out at a little girl. I know how hard he can hit, and I realise that the lashing out was a rather inappropriate attempt to interact, but it was my cue to quickly remove him. He was not happy. I met the mother of the little boy he had hurt previously on the way home, and she was lovely too. She thought my best choice was to leave him there to sort things out. Her concern was that he might misbehave in order to be collected early. However, the little girls at playgroup were becoming frightened of him, and that is simply not acceptable. Secondly, the Emperor loves the playgroup so bringing him home for quiet time instead of playtime is quite a punishment.

APPROPRIATE PUNISHMENT

This is hard. Toddlers forget very quickly what they have done. Association is one of your best tactics. By associating bad behaviour with removal of privileges or activities they enjoy you are most likely to stem bad behaviour. Of course you still need to discuss matters. I've never been in favour of 'Do as I say, because I say it.' However, you may have to reinforce discussion and explanation with appropriate punishment.

- Being made to say sorry lets children off the hook, when they need to be learning how to internalise right and wrong. There is nothing wrong with setting an example by saying sorry for your toddler, and encouraging them to apologise for a misdemeanour, but before the age of three understanding what an apology is about is difficult for them.

- Toddlers don't use logical reasoning. They learn through repetition. They may need to do something several times, with appropriate praise or punishment, before they understand.

- Tell your child clearly the behaviour you wish them to cease. "Do not yell," makes far more sense than "Calm down, you're being hyper," to a toddler.

- Keep rules to a minimum. All toddlers say 'no' a lot and have bad table manners. Safety rules need to be your priority. Rules about respecting other people and their property come next. And (sorry about this) rules about those annoying habits are actually the least important.

- Before age three natural consequences do not make a lot of sense. Often it is better to let a misbehaviour go (unless it concerns safety) than to reinforce that negative behaviour with attention.

- Distracting and diverting bad behaviour before it gets going helps.

- For serious offences parental disapproval and time-outs are most appropriate.

15TH OCTOBER

This was the Emperor's next scheduled playgroup day and I dropped him off with much trepidation. I had a chat with the playworkers, and raised my concern about simply coming down and removing him (how would he become socialised if he was constantly removed from other children?). We decided unless he did something massively wrong he would be given quiet time at a desk with an activity. I was a little concerned this might be just what he wanted, but it seemed a better option than removing him.

When I picked him up I heard he had spat twice, but this time he hadn't hit anyone so it was deemed a good day. He also had a little sticker that said 'I'm a whiz at puzzles'. Apparently, after receiving this, he had become as good as gold, and even behaved during story time. From this experience, and from talking to older, wiser grandmothers, I have deduced the second law of child control.

THE SECOND LAW

If the first law of child socialisation is Do not reward bad behaviour, the second law is Reward good behaviour. In practice the second rule is as important as the first not only in encouraging good behaviour, but even in preventing tantrums. ('Gosh, wasn't this a wonderful day without tantrums. Well done, you!') It sounds remarkably obvious, but I'm aware that I don't do this enough, and I don't think I am unusual in this. All parents may be pleased or grateful when their child is doing well, but we don't tend to dwell too much on this, unless it involves a major achievement. The human tendency seems to be to notice the bad and take for granted the good. I don't think it was a coincidence that my son's behaviour improved remarkably when he was given some extra positive attention from the playworkers. (And it's true; he is a whiz at puzzles.)

17TH OCTOBER

A big birthday for my mother, and the Emperor behaved beautifully; providing grandchildren makes any family affair a more exciting celebration.

POTTY TRAINING

I am aware entries in this area have been more fretful than practical. On the other hand there are countless books about potty training, and by the time your child is two it seems the average number given to parents by well meaning family and friends is roughly half a shelf full. However, as no book on toddlerhood would be complete without a section on potty training, here goes.

Basic concepts

- Don't start a child until they are ready.

- Don't be upset by backslidings, especially around difficult times (like the birth of a sibling).

- Don't be surprised if being dry at night takes longer.

- Don't make a fuss.

- Don't start until your child is capable of understanding and complying with simple commands.

- Don't start at a time when the household is in upheaval such as during a move or a busy holiday.

- If the exercise simply isn't working don't pursue it. Break off and begin again in about a month.

- Do always carry extra trousers/skirts (at least for the toddler) once you start.

- Do pay the extra for pull-up nappy trainer pants; you'll save on cleaning costs.

- Do ensure you always know where the nearest public toilets are when you are out (this may require reconnaissance).

Knowing when your child is ready

If you're lucky your child becomes aware of the process and starts telling you when they need a new nappy. They may also go into a corner, squat and grunt when they are 'doing a poo'. But it's a tricky process. The child needs to be aware of both what their body is doing, and what they need to do about it. In the early stages children cannot hold on for very long, and accidents can be quite distressing for them. Awareness of having done something comes well before the secondary learning of recognising the feeling that they need to go to the toilet. In both instances discoveries of bladder come before bowel.

What do you actually do?

Put aside your pride and allow your child to observe you on the toilet, and your partner or their siblings (if they are close in age).

Most children have a particular time for moving their bowels, and you can pre-empt this by putting them on the potty at the right time of day. Likewise you can put them on the potty after eating and drinking. Nothing much may happen for a while, and you need a lot of patience. There are quite a lot of good books for children about potty training. Chatting and sharing a picture book help more than you might imagine. Some parents also like to make up charts with stars for successful potty days. This is more effective if your child is nearer three and able to recognise when they need to pee or poo.

Remember if the parent is stressed and worried about potty training, then so will the child be. Chill!

What do you need?

There are all singing and all dancing potties and gizmos. Some even play musical tunes when a child performs. However, potty training existed before electronics, and expensive toys are not necessary. (I can't help but think avoiding such things may also save embarrassing accidents at concerts in later life.) A basic potty or a toilet seat (with accompanying podium so the child can reach the toilet) is all that is required. Wet wipes that can be flushed down the toilet do make it easier for children to learn to clean themselves, but are not essential.

Cool pants. Keeping pants in a special drawer before you begin, and explaining they are big girl/boy clothes, is exciting and encouraging. Take your child shopping to choose their own pants.

Designer training

By now you know how individual toddlers are. Potty training is another of those things that are different for all children. Some paragons are potty trained by 18 months, others not until they reach four. Some children will never use potties; they are so big by the time they are ready to train they will use a child toilet seat instead. One little girl I know refused completely to use her potty. In despair her parents left the potty in her room, and one day she started using it. (With my son this would only lead to a new and particularly unpleasant form of interior design.)

Remember when you were so worried about when they would say their first sentence, and now they talk all the time? Potty training is the same. All children have their own inner timetable. Our job is to provide instruction and love, and one day your patience will be rewarded by hearing the sound of that poo hitting the potty.

Key tips

- Don't punish accidents.

- Give your child lots of praise when they use the potty or toilet.

- Encourage the idea that using the potty is a fun and 'big' thing to do. (Most children love doing the things bigger children get to do.)

- Don't leave children in soiled clothes: they just get used to it and it makes everything harder.

- Potty picture books, potty games with dolls, special underwear all help.

- Older children (from around 30 months onwards) can do intense bare bottom sessions (anywhere from six hours to two days) where you spend time alone with the child (no TV or phone) in an uncarpeted area (or garden) playing games and keeping them near a potty. Give plenty to drink to encourage urinating. Keep the time upbeat and fun, and the child should become acutely aware of their body functions.

20TH OCTOBER

This week there is no playgroup, and I am realising how much I miss those three little two and a half hour slots of freedom.

BEING A MEMBER OF THE SECRET ARMY

I remain amazed at the morning world of childville. Walking along any street, entering any shop on a weekday morning, I am certain to come across more than one mother with her baby, and more and more likely to see lone fathers and children too. However, the majority of stay at home carers out doing their shopping remains women. We are a vast unnoticed army, dedicated to raising the next generation, unfunded, with no dental benefits past the first year, and certainly no sick leave.

23RD OCTOBER

The Emperor can now open the babygate on his bedroom, but
he waits until he is told he can. What's more he likes shutting
it behind him to secure his space. He cannot yet open the gate
on the living room, which is fortunate as it is upstairs and right
by the very steep stairs. The gallery kitchen is bolted shut with
a bolt so high I can barely reach.

ACCESS ALL AREAS

We would all like our children to grow up in huge, safe, rambling
houses, but few of us own these. Some children discover how to
open their babygates at two and younger, but I think there is a
good argument for leaving them in place. I've never liked the idea
of shutting a child in their room, but there are times when I am
doing something the Emperor cannot join in, and even if he could
he'd be happier playing with his toys than seeing his mother
curse and swear as she ruins her nails cleaning the bathroom.
Using gates to mark off space and as a request to stay in a particular room has worked very well for us. The Emperor knows he
can leave his room if he wishes and he also knows I am currently
unable to play with him. He makes a choice to obey me and stay.

25TH OCTOBER

The first day back at playgroup after the break was a success.
A very happy Emperor met me at the gate clutching a lollipop
and a cut-out flappy bat on a stick. He said goodbye nicely and
made no demur about leaving. He had also, according to senior playgroup worker, behaved perfectly. While it is early days
it does seem as if I am not raising Genghis Khan after all.

TODDLERHOOD IS A TIME OF CRISIS

I've just pinned sparkly bat (who is covered in glittery moonlight that sheds terribly) high above a picture in the Emperor's room. For 20 seconds it was as if his world had ended, but now he is happily drinking his milk and eating breadsticks. It's easy for parents to be suckered into this full on world of their little offspring. The reality is the two to three year is full of phases and, while some like toilet training and food fads last longer than others, generally your child is growing and learning at an astonishing rate.

With his playgroup problems I reacted as if my son was a 13 year old bully, a dyed in the wool bad boy, when in reality he was a tot taking the first steps in learning social interaction. The pain, worry and misery I expended over the last three weeks were immense and mostly unnecessary. On the one hand I know my reaction was positive, because it means I care very deeply about my son and desire strongly to help him grow up into a happy, socially integrated man. On the other hand, one of the other mothers at the toddler group, the mother of the boy my son wounded, is equally devoted a mother, but is completely laid back. This may be due to her being pregnant with her third child (all those wonderful calming hormones), but essentially she is a much calmer parent than I. So my advice for others and myself is to chill. Things are very rarely as bad as they initially appear, and loving your child is really the very best thing you can do for them. With time and attention other stuff works out.

27TH OCTOBER

I pick up the Emperor up from playgroup, and am told he has been good again. Then they drop the bombshell. It seems they forgot to tell me there is a Halloween party on Friday. How nice, I muse sentimentally, baby's first real other people party. And then she says, "He will come in costume, won't he?"

What do they think I am? The kind of mother who sews?

I foresee this is only the beginning, The future holds the requests of many teachers, play workers, scout leaders and their ilk, all asking me to make things. Fortunately, his father has artistic talent.

28TH OCTOBER

Today we started toddler gym properly. The Emperor wasn't perfectly behaved, but it was a lot better than the two trials he attended. It was unfortunate he had run through a number of puddles before we got there, making it look as if he had peed down his leg, but it didn't hold him back.

There is a fair range of big equipment for him to clamber over, but it's the songs and the balance beams that I really want him to try. He's a fearless climbing monkey, but patience and control are what we need to work on. Songs encourage him to follow the leaders, and do leader led actions rather than (as he did today) suddenly decide he wanted to be a cat, and miaow at everyone. He's strong enough to haul himself over all the equipment, but the balance beam (very low to the floor) forces him to stop and concentrate, and be aware of his body and how he is using it.

By the end of the lesson everyone knew his name. My son remains a noticeable personality. He's loud, and will chatter over the instructor. He'll rush for the equipment, and needs to be reminded to let others take turns. (In all fairness I have to say he was doing very well by the end of the lesson.

Although this did mean that occasionally he flopped down to a sitting position and sighed while waiting and watching a lesser mortal struggle through an exercise.)

I'm definitely the kind of mother who is relieved when another child misbehaves and draws the attention. However, I am training him well, and at the end of the class he went up to both instructors and said, "Thank you, Ladies. Bye-bye." This melted their hearts and he got two teddy bear stamps on his hand rather than just one.

MANNERS MAKETH TODDLER

Helping toddlers learn about taking turns, making an effort to thank instructors, saying thank you and goodbye at class, in shops and generally in the world has several effects. As well as showing them how to behave, it's amazing the strength of positive reactions people give to a toddler who acknowledges them and thanks them. To be honest the smiles and approval of strangers is often more weighty in the learning to behave stakes than Mama telling them yet again to behave.

Obviously I'm not advocating that you should encourage your child to interact with everyone (in a nicer world perhaps), but going up with you to thank, or say farewell to people in social situations is a wonderful positive enforcer. People who visit my house know my son will be brought in by one of us to say goodnight to our guests. He behaves beautifully, especially when it's getting near his birthday or Christmas.

It's also true that if you have a 'noticeable' child a sweet little thank you smoothes over a lot.

29ᵀᴴ OCTOBER

I drop Darth Vader off at his Halloween party, and ask senior playgroup worker if there is a chance of him getting an extra morning a week at least until Christmas because he enjoys the group so much. And I'm told no, because he isn't toilet trained, and they need the children to have some degree of independence. Now, leaving aside that I've frequently seen both workers on their knees helping very young children in the toilets and currently they need to do nothing for the Emperor, so he's hardly demanding in time, she took him on knowing he wasn't toilet trained, with the only comment being "We'll work with you on that." How exactly? By refusing to allow him to attend? He started at three mornings with the agreed expectation that this would go up to five.

She continues with, "He's had a very good week, but we don't know how he's going to behave." Let's see, my son has been there for less than three weeks, and because of three bad days he's been labelled trouble. She is also ignoring the fact that there are other kids who have difficulties, and a couple in particular who are known for scrapping.

I suspect she has not forgiven me for my first comments about safety and security. She's completely within her rights to refuse me, but she's cutting me no slack. His father is all for pulling him out at Christmas, telling them graphically what to do with their part time chair, and just letting him attend part time nursery. I'm torn selfishly because I had hoped we would keep a couple of playgroup mornings too, which would give me much more space, and less selfishly, because whatever I think of senior playworker, the Emperor loves it there.

RELATIONSHIPS WITH CHILDCARE PROFESSIONALS

I'd always imagined when my child went to playgroup, started school and so on I would enjoy my relationships with the people who taught and cared for him. There's quite a lot I can offer on the supportive front from extra toys for the playgroup (who are always short), to being on committees or running after school clubs. I see now this was a foolish dream. I'm not the kind of parent who does these things. I am the kind of parent who raises issues, asks questions, and refuses to bow their head and smile meekly. I am rather like the pupil I was at school. (How many others have reduced their headmaster to burying his head in his hands during their speech to the PTA?)

I've learned a big lesson with the playgroup about how wary childcare professionals are of difficult parents, and I shall tread gently when the Emperor goes to nursery and to school. When the parent falls out with the professionals there is a backlash on the child – even if it is only to refuse five extra mornings before Christmas at a playgroup he loves.

30TH OCTOBER

Yesterday, although it already feels like years ago, a relative died. Apart from feeling sad there hasn't been a great deal for me to do. This is a strange and uncomfortable place to be and now, of course, more practical issues need to be addressed. Do I take an almost three year old to a funeral? If I don't, do I go alone and stay away overnight? He already knows something is up, and Mama is upset. I can't help worrying that if she disappears for a day or more this will frighten him. While some children may be able to comprehend death, or at least that someone has gone away, one of the reasons the Emperor is so secure is his blind faith that everyone comes back.

A friend of mine lost her mother when her son was five years old. She explained that his grandmother had had to go away, and though she would have liked to have said goodbye, she wasn't able to do so. A few months later my friend, who had often had to go away for business conferences, was at her wits end with her son who would not let her out of his sight for more than a few hours at a time. Eventually, she got out of him the reason (which is entirely obvious with hindsight) that he was afraid that like Grandmother she too would be forced to go away forever.

DEATH

Two to three is too young to understand the finality of death and in many, many ways this is a blessing. Personally, I don't believe that children of this age, who are aware of other people's emotions and alert enough to ask questions, should be taken to funerals. Responses will range from "What's that box on the trolley – wheee!" to a tearful incomprehension of the sadness around. There is no doubt that life in the face of death is a positive experience, and seeing a happy, oblivious child running around a wake cheers many an ageing relative. But for me the emotional risks are too high. Yes, I will have to explain death to my son, but I am fortunate enough to have the choice not to explain it now. He will miss his relative, but the missing will be a gentle absence that fades over time, and is hopefully replaced by happy memories. When he finds the words to say where is x? Or realises he hasn't seen him for many, many months, then I will have to explain. But for now, I am permitting chocolate, letting

---

him play computer games (Harry Potter, at which he is terrible) and giving him many cuddles.

However, if you are in the unfortunate position where you have to explain death to a very young child, I would suggest that no matter what words you choose to use, you stress your love and your constant presence, and help the child feel as secure as possible. If it is a close relative then obviously the child will be very upset, but time and love are wonderful healers, and children are always that bit more robust than you expect.

- Don't be afraid to explain your spiritual beliefs to a child. It gives them the language to discuss what has happened.

- Reassure the child that the absence of a person is in no way their fault. Children often remember wishing or saying angry things, and may believe they drove someone away.

- Toddlers will need to be gently reminded someone is gone. It is very hard for them to understand death is permanent.

- Remember to take care of your own needs, and ask for help if you're having trouble dealing with your child's needs because of your own sadness.

31ST OCTOBER

"Where's my pumpkin?"

It's amazing what they learn at playgroup. Almost as amazing as how popular Halloween has become since I was a child. Fortunately the Emperor's luck was with me, and I managed to get the last pumpkin in town (which may sound like a song, but happens in this case to be the truth).

1ST NOVEMBER

Currently the Emperor is making his socks talk to him in that eerie high pitched voice he usually reserves for Stinky Bear. In a strange surreal way it makes sense, but then sleep last night was not in fashion. The Emperor has croup again.

ILLNESS

If you have a child who generally sleeps, it's amazing how easily you lose the ability to stay awake through day and night on the rare occasions you need to; an ability that was second nature only two, no almost three, years ago.

It is even more remarkable that despite illness and a night of little sleep your toddler will be as lively, or at least as demanding, as ever. If they aren't tearing around the room, then they will be clinging to your leg, and if still sick will grump at you all day.

Childhood illnesses raise a whole load of bugbears. Who looks after the child? Who takes time off work? (Working from home automatically elects you.) Be aware only those who also have children are going to understand.

At the time of writing the government is preparing to implement stages of their Parental Leave Directive. This is an excellent idea. However, there are limitations; being self-employed is an obvious one. But laws can only change so much. Regardless of whether the right to take time off to look after a sick child is enshrined in law, I confidently predict that if both parents work, employers will generally expect the woman to take time off, and that fathers who choose to do so in the middle of an important time will meet with negativity. I predict that if you are at the crux stage of a project, or in a key role, there will be a great deal of peer and career pressure on you, whether mother or father, not to take leave.

I have a very simple way to deal with such pressure. My suggestion is that you should do whatever your personal priorities dictate and, if your employers think differently, that this is exactly why tribunals were created. Having children isn't some strange hobby you've taken up; it's a requirement that some of us have children for the human species (and our society, not to mention professions, industries and pensions) to continue.

Never risk your child's health. You may have to call GPs in the middle of the night, you may have to piss off your boss, but taking care of your child is the priority. Everything else can wait.

5TH NOVEMBER

The playgroup situation is not getting any better. I decide to follow the softly, softly approach and ask senior playgroup worker how she potty trained her own children. Apparently for a month, she put them on the potty every 15 minutes.

Later, when they had the inevitable accidents, she left them a short while before changing them, so they could see how uncomfortable soiling themselves was. Somewhat startled I confer with the other mother on duty, who tells me she put her son on the potty every 20 minutes for a month.

Even in my wildest dreams there is no way I would have the time, patience or inclination to put my son on the potty or toilet four times an hour. To begin with we're talking of the most independent little boy ever; putting him anywhere causes a riot, and being asked to use the potty every few minutes would infuriate him even more than me.

I ask outside this little corner of the world. A friend, who has two children now aged eight and 10, tells me she toilet trained her children by explaining what they needed to do, and letting them get on with it. She said she had soggy carpets for a fortnight, and then it was sorted. A wise grandmother tells me that there is no point in forcing a child to potty train, and once the Emperor realises where other children are going, he'll train in a moment.

6TH NOVEMBER

The Emperor's playgroup runs in the morning only. I can get him either a morning or an afternoon place in nursery, but the nursery is curriculum led and the playgroup is, well, social play. The playgroup does have a structure, and they are particularly good at getting the children to do arts and crafts. However, all I have read suggests morning is the time children learn. This has now been confirmed with my insider source ex-nursery teacher. Essentially, it matters a whole lot less what children do in the afternoon.

This means I am still going to be doing the ridiculous juggling act I am at the moment, where I spend time at home working, and being interrupted every 10 minutes by my son, until pressure overwhelms me and I cave and start playing with him.

It's not a good way to function. Whenever I am playing with him I worry about my writing, and whenever I am writing I worry I am not giving him enough attention. I am also becoming convinced no one else in the world is doing the same as me. (Although rationally I know this is untrue.)

THE PARENTING DILEMMA

Even if you are fortunate enough to choose to be a stay at home parent, and dedicate all your time to your children, sometimes it's going to pall. If you have to stay at home then it's even harder. If you choose to go out to work, you'll always wonder if you're doing the right thing; and if you have to go out to work, then you're going to wonder even more.

I'm making a choice not to work full time and not to put him in care full time. It does mean that there are days when I feel I am doing more jobs than anyone else on the face of the planet, and sometimes as a stay home and working parent, this is true. Accordingly there will be times when both of us wish we had things differently, but for me (and him) this is the best compromise.

You need to find your own.

7TH NOVEMBER

We're fast approaching the end of this diary, and I'm finding the entries are coming faster than ever. There seems to be so much to say, and so little space left. One topic I haven't covered is my ongoing illness. I have mild MS which means I tire easily, and occasionally have bouts of pain. I am also a long term sufferer from depression, which I deal with through activity, meditation and knowledge rather than medication. It's certainly true that having an understanding GP, as well as being a trained psychotherapist myself, helps enormously. The MS is more difficult because I never know what the future is going to bring; whether I will be able to maintain this level of health, and also whether I will be able to keep up with my increasingly active toddler.

PARENTAL CHRONIC ILLNESS AND TODDLERS

I don't think having long term health issues makes you a poor or lesser parent. It's amazing what you can handle and cope with when dealing with a toddler. This year is one of the hardest you will ever face, but it is also one of the most rewarding. If you have extra health issues to cope with then it will be harder, but finding your way through will make the rewards all the sweeter. Explain things to your toddler in ways they will understand. My son has had to come to terms with the fact Mama will always tire faster than Dada, and that she cannot play all the lifting games that Dada can. However Mama is a great teller of stories and a world renowned hugger.

Your health doesn't affect your ability to love, and loving your toddler is right up there with feeding, sheltering and protecting in the scales of important things parents do.

9TH NOVEMBER

I've cleared it with the playgroup to take in a cake for him tomorrow. Then I'm told that the committee meeting has been moved yet again. I think if the Emperor gets a morning nursery place, then it will be bye-bye to the playgroup, which is a shame because he enjoys it so much. He loves the arts and crafts, and the running around in the big space, but intellectually he needs that structured curriculum in the morning. We shall have to see what the new nursery can offer me.

A friend of mine recently commented that her main problem with dealing with people who work with small children is that after a while they treat everyone as if they are a small child. I wonder if throwing a tantrum would work?

10TH NOVEMBER

Today we are three. From having little language my son now regularly commands his mother to "Sssh! Don't talk", "Be careful!", and even advises me (as I have never advised him) "Don't dance, Mama!". It seems I am already embarrassing. He has taught all my friends to say 'Maybe not' instead of the more confrontational 'no'. He turns his own telly on and off. He's not potty trained, but he is more or less able to dress himself.

Today has been a day of ups and downs. It was lovely that all the children at his playgroup sang him Happy Birthday and shared his cake. It was less lovely that I arrived mid-morning with the cake to find not only the gate onto the road open, but also the front door. Most of the children were sitting in another room to have a story, but my son had been allowed to stay in the main room. When I voiced my concern, it was again brushed off, with an assurance someone was just fetching the gate key. It would take less than 10 seconds for my son to exit the front door and end up in the road. I am coming to terms with the realisation I cannot make these people listen to me. Nothing has ever gone badly wrong, so they assume it never will. I am dealing with feelings of despair at losing my free time, anger at the playgroup and concern I am an overprotective mother. My horror at the open doors definitely put a damper on my day.

The rest of the day goes well, with a further cake in the evening, and presents spread throughout the day so he didn't open everything at once.

11ᵀᴴ NOVEMBER

Yesterday's Birthday Boy was very unhappy this morning. Cried getting dressed. Cried putting on his shoes. Cried when we left the house. Cried and leant against the front door. Cried so much I thought there was no point taking him to his gym class. Cried even more when he was taken inside. Banged his head off everything he could find to show me how upset he was. Finally cried himself to sleep. Woke up 15 minutes later to cry some more, before being appeased by cake and children's TV.

So this is post-birthday syndrome.

THE TWELVE MONTH REVIEW

MY GOALS

1 By the time he is three the Emperor will be eating a healthy mixed diet without complaint, and pudding bribes will be a thing of the past.

The Emperor is a good height and weight for his age, so despite his lack of vegetable eating, I'm going to give us a 7/10.

2 Nappies will be a dim memory, with all bodily waste products going in the loo, without having to go through the hell of pottydom.

If I've learnt anything it's not to fret about potty training. Encourage your child by allowing them to train in their own time. So I'm putting up a score of n/a

3 Every night the Emperor will go down for at least 10 hours of undisturbed rest.

Bedtime is much more regular now, and he sleeps well. 9/10

4 As mother I will continually strive to provide entertainment and activities suitable for the Emperor's developing mind and body (which includes ethically correct selection of toys and television programs).

This has been very tiring, but I think we did OK. 8/10

5 I will begin the socialisation process of the Emperor by finding him other children to play with, and cease surrounding him totally with servile adults.

In terms of stress the playgroup was a disaster, but the Emperor enjoyed going there, and did learn a lot about socialising with other children. Toddler gym and swimming sessions also helped. 7/10

6 At the end of the year, the Emperor will be able to give his real name and address when asked, and will be fluent in conversational adult-speak.

He still won't give his address, but he can recognise it. He happily chats away and frequently issues me with commands. 9/10

7 I will ensure that the Emperor's surroundings are safe, and that we never have another occurrence of the collapsed babygate and the stairs.

He did fall down the stairs, but he was and remains remarkably fit and healthy. 7/10

8 I will undertake to school the Emperor in the ways of acceptable behaviour without resorting to corporal punishment, or anything that may entail long term therapy (for either of us) at a later date.

This is a difficult one to score. He accidentally wounded another child. He still has tantrums. He is learning manners and to speak politely to people. He's trying hard, and despite being a bit of wild child, we are working well towards helping him manage his emotions. 8/10

9 I will not work full time. I will devote huge amounts of each day to the caring of the Emperor and his environs, but I will also write, study and achieve a minimal level of social life.

I did manage to write this book, a play, and a novel this year. I didn't get a social life, and I did focus intently on the Emperor. I think he did fine. I'm not so sure about myself. 7/10

10 I will not be a sucker for the Emperor's huge blue topaz eyes or other formidable weapons in his armoury of manipulation and cajolement.

I do withstand him when it is in his best interests, and I'm getting better at this. 6/10

THE EMPEROR'S GOAL

1 To bend the known universe to his will.

We're even. 5/10

THE FINAL ANNUAL REPORT

Looking back over the year

When I first reread this diary I seriously thought about changing huge chunks of it. I felt I made my son sound like a monster, which he is not. However, while I was considering this option I went on a bus journey on which I met a mother and her toddler. During the 20 minute journey the child kicked, screamed, tried to climb out of his buggy and generally tortured his mother. The stares and comments from the rest of the passengers became increasingly unpleasant. As I was getting off, I stopped and said to her, "He sounds just like my son," The poor woman almost burst into tears. "Thank God," she said, "it isn't just me."

So while neither her child nor mine are monsters, they do occasionally transmute into demons. This is what toddlers do.

Hygiene

The Emperor isn't toilet trained but he is becoming interested and *if I've learnt anything it's not to sweat stuff that children will naturally do in their own time.* He loves brushing his teeth, washing his hands, and if I gave him the number of baths he wanted, he'd never be out of the water.

Feeding

I do wish the Emperor had never tasted chocolate, but he is gradually showing signs of being a little more adventurous with food.

As long as your child is growing well and is a good height and weight for their age, then toddler's choice is an acceptable way to work. Do continue to offer a variety of food, and gradually you'll find chil-

dren do expand their tastes as long as you don't make a fuss about things.

Social skills

This is one area where the Emperor is doing amazingly well. His language has advanced in leaps and bounds, and mixing with other children is helping him enormously. Being places where he wasn't the most important child to everyone there has helped him develop a public persona, even if this has boosted his armoury of manipulation skills.

Play

The Emperor is well into the arena of imaginative play. Although he likes company he will also withdraw into his own world where his toys are actors and he is the director (and often sound and stunt co-ordinator too).

Toddlers need time to play alone, as well as time with other children and family.

Protection

When your child is a baby they seem like a fragile little mite in a big harsh world, and the duty to protect them is awesome. When that baby turns into a normal toddler who rushes out to meet all and any danger, it is easy to be become overwhelmed by fear.

It's been clear during this diary that I have issues with my local playgroup. Due to my safety concerns, I will remove the Emperor when he attends nursery next year. I am struggling with my fears and trying to find a perspective that allows for the reality that no one is ever going to treat my child well enough as far as I am concerned. We live in a world full of risks, and as parents we have to make decisions. This is never going to get easier.

THE MOTHER'S REVIEW

I have found this year as wonderful as I have found it hard. I don't think I have ever experienced such a testing and challenging time. I wouldn't have missed it for the world.

WHERE DO WE GO FROM HERE?

The nursery turned out to be wonderful, and exactly what he needed. The Emperor has fitted in well. The staff tell me he is a very bright boy, who is interested in everything. He loves it there and is learning more every day.

As four beckons I know there will be a whole host of new challenges to meet – and some old ones too (food and toilet training), but this has been a good year. The Emperor and I have grown together. Whatever happens, I know we will meet the future hand in hand. He knows his father and I will always be there for him, and we know caring for him and loving him is the greatest and the most rewarding challenge life can offer us.

CONTACT US

You're welcome to contact White Ladder Press if you have any questions or comments for either us or the author. Please use whichever of the following routes suits you.

Phone: 01803 813343

Email: enquiries@whiteladderpress.com

Fax: 01803 813928

Address: White Ladder Press, Great Ambrook, Near Ipplepen, Devon TQ12 5UL

Website: www.whiteladderpress.com

WHAT CAN OUR WEBSITE DO FOR YOU?

If you want more information about any of our books, you'll find it at www.whiteladderpress.com. In particular you'll find extracts from each of our books, and reviews of those that are already published. We also run special offers on future titles if you order online before publication. And you can request a copy of our free catalogue.

Many of our books also have links pages, useful addresses and so on relevant to the subject of the book. You'll also find out a bit more about us and, if you're a writer yourself, you'll find our submission guidelines for authors. So please check us out and let us know if you have any comments, questions or suggestions.

FANCY ANOTHER GOOD READ?

If you've enjoyed this book, how about reading another of our books for helping busy parents have an easier and more enjoyable time with their children? *The Art of Hiding Vegetables Sneaky ways to feed your children healthy food* does just what it says on the tin.

It's hard enough getting your children to eat two or three portions of fresh fruit and vegetables a day, let alone the recommended five. But have you tried subterfuge? This book is packed with ideas for hiding the fresh food or dressing it up so that even a small child will be seduced into eating it. With tips and suggestions for meals from breakfast to supper, plus snacks, lunchboxes, drinks and parties, this practical and realistic book is designed to help busy parents introduce a healthier diet for their children without spending more money or taking up time they don't have.

Here's a taster of what you'll find in *The Art of Hiding Vegetables*. If you like the look of it and want to order a copy you can use the order form in the back of the book, call us on 01803 813343 or order online at www.whiteladderpress.com.

"As a working mother, this is just the book I need. It's packed with great ideas which are clever, practical and simple to use."

Melinda Messenger

THE ART OF HIDING VEGETABLES

Sneaky ways to feed your children healthy food

PARENT-TO-PARENT IDEAS, TIPS AND TRICKS

Almost every parent has at least one way of getting their child to eat fruit and vegetables, from plain old bribery to far more sneaky measures.

Here is a selection of the best ideas, gathered from nutritionists and chefs but mostly from ordinary parents:

DISGUISE WITH CHEESE

If your child likes cheese, and most do, try vegetables in cheese sauce (broccoli, cauliflower, onions, garlic etc) or grated cheese, melted if preferred, over the top.

FONDUE!

Have fun with a savoury sauce like cheese or spicy tomato and either raw or very lightly cooked vegetables. Similarly, a sweet or chocolate sauce can help a whole load of fruit go down without any problem.

USE THE WATER

Always try to save the water in which you cook your green vegetables. Lots of vitamins leak into the water when the vegetables are cooking and rather than throwing this away, use it to make gravy or add to soup and stew.

WAIT UNTIL THEY HAVE VISITORS

The best time to try something new is when your children have friends over for a meal. Whether it is a main course with well hidden vegetables or a pudding consisting mainly of fruit, the friends will not know that this is different from the norm. If other children eat the food without question, yours should too. Don't hover, watch or comment – just serve the food and disappear.

PEEL AND CHOP FRUIT FOR THEM

Children, lovely as they are, can be lazy when it comes to eating. Whether it is peeling an orange or chewing their way through a whole apple (including skin), usually they just can't be bothered. For pudding, snacks or supper, they are much more likely to eat fruit if you do the hard work. Serve it immediately after preparation – brown apples and soggy strawberries are not appetising.

You could include:

- Peeled bananas, chopped into chunks
- A couple of peeled and segmented satsumas
- A few strawberries, washed, dried and without the stalks
- A handful of grapes, washed and dried
- An apple or pear, peeled and chopped

- Some cherries, washed and dried without the stalks (removing the stones is a little extreme, unless your children are young enough to choke on them)
- Sweet oranges, cut into quarters or eighths with the skin on – children love to suck the juice whilst making funny faces with the orange skin over their teeth
- Small, ripe apricots, washed, cut in half with stones removed
- Kiwi fruit – peeled and sliced or cut into quarters, or halved so they can be scooped out and eaten with a teaspoon
- Slices of mango, papaya, and pineapple add a tropical taste for a refreshing change

START WITH ONE

If your child says that they do not like a certain vegetable, maybe they don't, but maybe they have not even tried it. When serving the vegetable with a family meal, put just one (or one teaspoon) of this vegetable on their plate – yes, even one pea. If they comment, pretend that it slipped onto the plate 'by mistake'. You may need to do this several times before they eat it, but before you know it they may be asking for more.

BARGAINING

Make a meal with three types of vegetable. If they complain or attempt to leave them all, make out you are doing them a favour by letting them leave two if they eat one.

If they protest that they don't want to try vegetables or fruit, agree with them that if they try something 10 times and still don't like it they will not have to eat it again.

GET THEM TO COUNT

Explain to your children about the health benefits of fruit and vegetables – their school should be reinforcing this as part of the curriculum. At the end of the day (just occasionally, not every day) ask them in the evening how many portions of fruit and vegetables they have eaten that day. Praise them or give a small reward (a gold star, 10p) if they have had five or over. The Rainbow Food Activity Chart can help with this.

BRIBE THEM!

Not every parent agrees with bribery, but you may find it works and it can help in the short term to get them used to new foods. Offer them something as a reward for eating up all their vegetables or finishing a plate of fruit, but not every day or every mealtime. The danger is they will expect rewards for eating vegetables, even when they get older. A new bike or a holiday with friends is no fair exchange for your teenager eating their carrots...

SALAD

Start adding a little salad to finger food – sandwiches, chips, pizza or nuggets. Just two or three chunky cucumber slices, a cherry tomato or two and a few little carrot sticks can make quite a difference to the nutritional content of a child's meal or snack. Don't comment if they leave some but give the same amount each time – the amount that they eat should gradually increase.

STIR-FRY

Many children love beansprouts, not least because they look like worms. Stir-fry for just a couple of minutes (not until they go soggy) with finely sliced carrots, peppers and onions and serve with rice or noodles. Speaking of rice, add chopped herbs, finely chopped onions, peas and sweetcorn to your fried rice – delicious!

CALL IT SOMETHING INTERESTING

Young children can be persuaded to try almost anything if they like the sound of it. Pirate's pie, fairy swirl, fisherman's lunch, giant's mountains, princess picnic, etc.

ORANGE MASH

Instead of boring mashed potato with their sausages or on top of shepherd's pie, make the mash orange with carrots, swede and sweet potato – it looks and tastes more interesting and a little cheese can be added to improve the taste.

GARNISH EVERYTHING

Whether you grow your own on the kitchen windowsill or buy them fresh or growing in pots, a sprinkling of finely chopped herbs in every savoury dish can contribute to the daily intake of vitamins. Most have a subtle flavour and your children will soon get so used to seeing a garnish they will not even notice after a while.

ROAST EVERYTHING

Don't just stick to roast potatoes with your roast dinner. Roasting carrots, peppers, onions, sweet potatoes, parsnips, tomatoes, mushrooms and baby sweetcorn can make a great meal with minimum meat.

BATTER IT

A simple batter can transform dull food into an exciting snack. Cut fruit or vegetables into bite-size pieces and dip into batter mix then fry in olive oil or butter. Serve battered vegetables with salsa, mayonnaise or ketchup and battered fruit with honey, puréed fruit or melted chocolate.

GROW YOUR OWN

If you have a garden and just a little time, growing your own fruit and vegetables with the help of your children will not only educate them about where food comes from but encourage them to eat what they grow. It is much more interesting for children to eat peas they have picked and shelled for dinner or to take an apple picked from a tree in their own garden in their school lunch box. Even if you don't have a garden, a few herbs or small fruits (eg strawberries) can be grown in pots. Children also love growing their own cress from seed in little pots with cotton wool at the bottom.

GO PICKING

If you don't have room in your garden to grow fruit or vegetables, or don't have the time or inclination, pick-your-own is a good alternative.

Farms and market gardens everywhere use pick-your-own as a way to offer cheaper produce and also save on labour costs. Make an outing to pick strawberries and take a picnic to have with them afterwards – this is an enjoyable and cheap day out. Vegetable picking too can be interesting for young children, especially if they are allowed to wash and prepare them at home for eating or freezing. Label them with the child's name 'Lizzie's peas, September 2004' or 'Jake's raspberries, July 2005' – this will not only remind them of a nice day out but encourage them to eat up when they are served.

CHEAT WITH BABY FOOD

If your child is averse to lumps, jars of baby food are a great way to add nutritious ingredients to many dishes. They are also now low in salt and sugar and many contain just puréed fruit or vegetables. Add vegetable baby food to soup and sauces – fruit baby food can be added to yogurt, cream, custard or ice cream.

KIDS&Co

"Ros Jay has had a brilliant idea, and what is more she has executed it brilliantly. **KIDS & CO** is the essential handbook for any manager about to commit the act of parenthood, and a thoroughly entertaining read for everyone else"
JOHN CLEESE

WHEN IT COMES TO RAISING YOUR KIDS, YOU KNOW MORE THAN YOU THINK.

So you spent five or ten years working before you started your family? Maybe more? Well, don't waste those hard-learned skills. Use them on your kids. Treat your children like customers, like employees, like colleagues.

No, really.

Just because you're a parent, your business skills don't have to go out of the window when you walk in throughthe front door. You may sometimes feel that the kids get the better of you every time, but here's one weapon you have that they don't: all those business skills you already have and they know nothing about. Closing the sale, win/win negotiating, motivational skills and all the rest.

Ros Jay is a professsional author who writes on both business and parenting topics, in this case simultaneously. She is the mother of three young children and stepmother to another three grown-up ones.

£6.99

Full Time Father

HOW TO SUCCEED AS A STAY AT HOME DAD

"At last, a hands-on, amusing and above all realistic guide for dads who have given up work to bring up their children. What makes this book so rewarding is that it is written by a father who has been there, seen it and done it."
Nick Cavender, Chairman, HomeDad UK

So your partner earns more than you do?
You've been made redundant? You hate the job?
Being a full time dad can make a lot of sense.

But isn't it a bit weird? Actually no; it's a growing trend. Nearly one in ten fathers in the UK now takes the main responsibility for looking after the kids, often full time.

It's a big decision though. What will your mates think? Will you ever get a decent job again? Won't you miss the cut and thrust of the office? And won't you go stark staring mad without any mental stimulation too sophisticated for a toddler? It's not just you, either. It's the whole family set up. Who wears the trousers? Who controls the family purse? And does it mean you have to clean the house and do the shopping, too?

Full Time Father is written by a stay at home dad and draws on his survey of other 'homedads' as well as on his own experience. It examines all the key issues, passes on masses of valuable tips and advice, and lets the reader know what to expect – both good and bad – should they decide to become a homedad themselves.

£9.99

Recipes *for* Disaster*s*

How to turn kitchen cock-ups
into magnificent meals

"Methinks 'twould have spared me much grief had I had this cunning volume to hand when I burnt those cursèd cakes." *King Alfred the Great*

It was all going so well... friends for lunch, guests for dinner, family for Christmas. You're planning a delicious meal, relaxed yet sophisticated, over which everyone can chat, drink a glass of fine wine and congratulate you on your culinary talent.

And then, just as you were starting to enjoy it – disaster! The pastry has burnt, the pudding has collapsed or the terrine won't turn out. Or the main ingredient has been eaten by the cat. Or perhaps it's the guests who've buggered everything up: they forgot to mention that they're vegetarian (you've made a beef bourguignon). Or they've brought along a friend (you've only made six crème brûlées).

But don't panic. There are few kitchen cock-ups that can't be successfully salvaged if you know how. With the right attitude you are no longer accident-prone, but adaptable. Not a panicker but a creative, inspirational cook.

Recipes for Disasters is packed with useful tips and ideas for making sure that your entertaining always runs smoothly (or at least appears to, whatever is going on behind the scenes). Yes, you still can have a reputation as a culinary paragon, even if it is all bluff.

£7.99

OUT OF YOUR TOWNIE MIND

THE REALITY BEHIND THE DREAM OF COUNTRY LIVING

"Richard Craze yanks the rose-tinted spectacles from the rural idyll and tramples them in the mud. The result is cheeky but charming — a kind of Feel-the-Fear-But-Do-It-Anyway for wannabe downshifters." **Hugh Fearnley-Whittingstall**

We all have our own fantasy of what life in the country will be like. But are we right? Is it all roses round the door, or are they really brambles?

So you're finally sick of city life. You close your eyes and dream of living in the country – all that space, and wonderful views. Going for long walks and coming home to an open fire, bringing your children up healthy and safe and being part of a community. Maybe you have visions of baking cakes on an Aga, keeping your own hens and handknitting your own yoghurt…

But will it really be like that?

Out of Your Townie Mind takes the most popular dreams of rural life that townies have (based on a survey of aspiring country dwellers) and lays the real facts on the line. Does a big garden really give you more space to enjoy the country, or just create so much work you never have time to enjoy it? Will a house in the woods be a private haven of wildlife, your own nature reserve on the doorstep… or is it just dark, damp and a recipe for endless gutter clearing?

Out of Your Townie Mind shows you how, with a bit of forethought, you can get the very best out of country living by avoiding the pitfalls other townies stumble into.

£7.99

Order form

You can order any of our books via any of the contact routes on page 168, including on our website. Or fill out the order form below and fax it or post it to us.

We'll normally send your copy out by first class post within 24 hours (but please allow five days for delivery). We don't charge postage and packing within the UK. Please add £1 per book for postage outside the UK.

Title (Mr/Mrs/Miss/Ms/Dr/Lord etc) _____

Name _____

Address _____

_____

Postcode _____

Daytime phone number _____

Email _____

No. of copies	Title	Price	Total £
Postage and packing £1 per book (outside the UK only):			
TOTAL:			

Please either send us a cheque made out to White Ladder Press Ltd or fill in the credit card details below.

Type of card ☐ Visa ☐ Mastercard ☐ Switch

Card number _____

Start date (if on card) _____ Expiry date _____ Issue no (Switch) _____

Name as shown on card _____

Signature _____

INDEX